Past-into-Present Series

DRINK

Sheila Ferguson

Head of the History Department
Peckham Girls' School, London

B T BATSFORD LTD London & Sydney

First published 1975
© Sheila Ferguson 1975

ISBN 0 7134 2901 1

Printed by
Anchor Press, Tiptree, Essex

for the Publishers
B T Batsford Ltd, 4 Fitzhardinge Street, London W1H 0AH
23 Cross Street, Brookvale, NSW 2100, Australia

To my mother

Acknowledgments

The author and Publishers would like to thank the following for their kind permission to reproduce copyright illustrations on the pages mentioned: the Radio Times Hulton Picture Library for pages 6, 7, 9, 11, 13, 14, 17 (top and bottom), 19, 21, 22, 23, 26 (top) 29, 30, 34, 35, 39 (top and right), 40, 47 (left and right), 48, 49, 52, 67, 71, 73 (left and right), 77, 79 (top),80; the Trustees of the British Museum for page 8; the Mansell Collection for pages 26 (bottom), 31, 33, 43 (bottom), 58 (top) 66, 75; Mary Evans Picture Library for pages 43 (top), 44, 53, 54, 58 (bottom), 63, 64, 68; Bovril Ltd for page 56; the Guinness Museum for page 59; Wayland Picture Library for page 69; Keystone Press Agency for pages 79 (bottom), 85 (left), 87 (right), 89 (left and right); the Milk Marketing Board for pages 82 (top), 87 (left); Henry Grant for page 85 (right). The other illustrations appearing in this book are the copyright of the Publishers.

Contents

The Illustrations

1. Drink in Early Times

The first men on earth probably lived, say the geologists, some 500,000 years ago. They were hunters and food gatherers, and slaked their thirst like the other animals — from rivers, streams, springs and pools. Water was a necessity of life, so man learned to regulate his movements around a reliable water supply, just as he followed the herds of animals that provided his food. At first he lay on the ground and drank straight from the water or cupped his hands as a drinking vessel. Then he found out that there were many convenient natural containers to drink from, such as sea-shells, coconuts, gourds, the egg-shells of large birds and even human skulls. As his brain and his skills developed, man began to fashion vessels of pottery for his food and drink, and later he made pots of metal.

The First Fermented Drinks

After a time our ancestors discovered the pleasures of fermented drink. Alcohol is made naturally when single-celled living substances called yeasts come into contact with sugar. Probably some grapes gathered for eating were overlooked and left in a container where they began to ferment; the bubbling and seething liquid was found to have an agreeable warming effect and to promote cheerfulness. What started as an accidental discovery could be repeated as a deliberate process; the manufacture of wine had begun.

In the same way the honey which early man eagerly collected from the nests of bees probably got mixed with water, and the wild yeasts produced an alcoholic drink which was a kind of mead. Similarly naturally fermenting apples led to the making of the first cider. All these fermented drinks were well-known in Persia and the early civilizations of the Near East more than 10,000 years ago.

After many thousands of years of life as nomadic hunters, some groups of men began to settle down and become farmers. They cultivated some of the plants they had previously collected growing wild, and domesticated the animals they had once hunted. These settlements occurred first in the great river valleys of the Tigris, Euphrates, Nile, Indus and Ganges where the climate and soil were especially favourable. Milk and whey from cattle, mares, sheep and goats (though primarily regarded as food) were now alternative drinks which could be stored in the earthenware pots men had learned to make. They harvested wheat and barley and used the flour to make a kind of porridge and hard flat cakes; then they discovered yeast and this enabled them to make the bread rise and to brew ale, a fermented drink made from barley.

Roman and Anglo-Saxon Britain

When the Romans came to Britain they found that the British tribal chiefs imported wine from the Continent and kept substantial stocks of it. Great wine storage jars in the Britons' burial chambers show how highly it was valued. At their feasts the Britons drank their wine lavishly and undiluted, and got noisily drunk. The Romans, on the other hand, drank their wine mixed with water and often warmed. After the Roman Conquest, the amount of imported wine rose sharply, and there were regular shipments from Bordeaux, Spain and Germany. Wine was the drink for all elegant social occasions. A rough cheap wine was part of the Roman soldier's ration, though local beer which was cheaper was even more popular.

Along their new straight roads, the Romans built *tabernae* (taverns) for the refreshment of travellers, where both wine and ale were available. The Romans imported hops for flavouring the beer, so producing a more bitter beer.

1 (*Opposite*) A painting on a fifth-century BC Greek drinking cup shows a lady pouring out wine for a warrior just about to set off to the wars.

2 (*Above*) Saxon gentlemen with their personal knives and drinking vessels, made from cows' horns, ready for a feast.

However, when the Romans left, the Britons reverted again to ale without hops. Ale was on its way to becoming the national drink of Britain, though competition with the honey brews of mead and metheglin and with imported wines was to continue for centuries.

The Angles, Saxons, Jutes and Vikings who invaded Britain after the Romans came from countries where the vine could not flourish. They were great drinkers of ale and cider, and used the horns of their cattle as drinking vessels. One of their favourite contests was to empty a horn at one go. This was no mean feat since a horn could contain as much as a quart of beer (1.1 litres).

Each family made its own ale, using various herbs for flavouring, a favourite one being nettle. Ale was almost the only drink for ordinary people, and was drunk at all meals by men, women and children. The process of brewing ale included boiling the liquid which no doubt made it a safe drink in places where the water was unclean. Ale-houses also brewed their own beer, and the Saxon kings made the first laws to regulate brewing activities in Britain.

Mead was another favourite drink of the Anglo-Saxons. In their literature, such as *Beowulf*, mead is mentioned as the drink of kings and noblemen. It was especially favoured in Wales where it was known as metheglin, and was made of fermented honey and water and such spices and herbs as cloves, ginger, rosemary, hyssop and thyme. In the tenth century King Howell laid down rules for its manufacture. When it was found that beeswax made excellent candles, medieval monks began to keep innumerable hives; and since they had a lot of honey, they made mead as well as candles.

7

2. Medieval and Tudor Drinks

Standards for Ales and Beers

After the Norman Conquest (1066) the brewing of ale continued to be a duty of medieval housewives, but it was also steadily becoming something of an industry. Abbeys and monasteries had breweries which catered for their own communities, and also for travellers to whom they gave hospitality. Farmers' wives or servants produced beer, for the family and for the farm labourers. Soon, just as bakeries began to take on the daily task of baking bread, so breweries began to produce ale for sale. By the reign of Henry IV (1399-1413), a guild, 'the Mistery of Free Brewers', existed in London, and in 1437 Henry VI granted a charter to the Worshipful Company of Brewers. This gave them the right to control 'the mistery and processes connected with brewing any kind of malt liquor in the City of London and its suburbs for ever.' This right still exists today.

Cooks in the Middle Ages used large amounts of spices to make palatable the salted or not-too-fresh meat and fish, and this led to a huge national thirst. Ale (or cider and perry in the apple and pear growing parts of the country) was the

main drink of all classes. The poorer people drank ale at all meals; the more well-to-do drank it at breakfast and during the day, but drank mead or wine with their evening meal. Some brews may have been three times as strong as the beer we drink today, but much of it was probably weaker, being a sweet, malty drink without the bitter flavour and aroma provided by hops. English ale had a good reputation abroad, and in 1157 Thomas-a-Becket made a gift of Canterbury ale to the King of France. A writer at the time described this ale as 'decocted from choice, fat grain . . . a drink most wholesome, clear of dregs, rivalling wine in colour and surpassing it in flavour.'

There were, however, many petitions to the King and to the town councils about the adulteration of ale; since it was such an important item in the national diet, action was taken. The Magna Carta signed by King John in 1215, which aimed at curbing the powers of the monarch, also included a statement on standard measures for ale and wine. The Assize of Bread and Ale introduced by Henry III in 1267 controlled the price and quality of these two staple items. Regulations continued for the next 300 years. Maximum retail prices were regularly laid down and varied according to the price of barley. Enforcement of quality, though, was difficult when there were no reliable standard weights and measures. In 1276 the first ale 'conners' were appointed in London to keep a check on the quality of ale. Brewers were restrained from making more than two kinds of beer, 'strong' and 'double', so that prices could more easily be fixed by law, but enforcement of these laws proved difficult. During the reign

4 (*Above*) Some of the processes involved in the brewing of beer, including the growing and picking of hops.

3 (*Opposite*) Medieval cooks get out meat which has been stored in casks of brine. Pepper, ginger, cinnamon, cloves, nutmeg, saffron, cummin and other spices helped to disguise the taste of the stale and salted meat or fish.

of Queen Elizabeth I (1558-1603) there was some anxiety expressed about the effects of drinking strong ales, which were given such exotic names as 'doble-doble', 'dagger ale', 'huff cup', 'dragon's milk' or 'merry-go-round', and were a good deal stronger than our very strongest beers today.

Hops

In the fifteenth century hops began to be used again for the brewing of beer in England. Hops give beer a bitter flavour and are useful both as an antiseptic and a preservative. They were imported from what is now Czechoslovakia and reached England via Holland and Belgium. This connection with the Netherlands can be seen in the old names for casks still used today — firkin (9 gallons or 41 litres), and kilderkin (18 gallons or 82 litres). Hops had been used during the Roman occupation and were well-known in Continental countries. Their reintroduction into England met with some resistance, and for a time Henry VII banned their use. Restrictions were removed in 1523 but some people were still critical. Andrew Boorde, bishop, doctor and dietician, spoke well of ale made from water, malt and yeast, 'the natural drink of an Englishman', but thought beer made from water, malt and hops was 'the natural drink of a Dutchman'. 'Ale maketh a man strong', said Boorde, but beer 'doth make him fat and doth inflate the belly.' Ale should be 'fresh and clear' he said, 'not ropy or smoky, nor must it have any weft or layce'; it should not be drunk under five days old as 'new ale is unwholesome, sour and dead ale, good for no man.' By Tudor times, barley was being widely grown in East Anglia to be brewed into beer for the London market. Hops were produced in Kent and Essex to supply the flavour for the beer.

Ale-houses and Taverns

From very early times there was a need to provide refreshment for travellers as well as for local inhabitants. The first ale-houses, rough mud huts with thatched roofs, established themselves along well-used routes, to supply the traveller with home-brewed ale and cider. The Saxon King Ethelred inflicted penalties for disorder in ale-houses, and later taverns had to shut down when the curfew sounded at night.

One of the duties of early abbeys and monasteries, too, was to house and provide refreshment for pilgrims and other travellers. Guest houses were attached to all these religious establishments, but soon the number of people needing shelter proved larger than the monasteries could accommodate, and so annexes were built. Often the annexes were called the 'New Inn'. Thus there were two kinds of inns, both of which served ale; one was simply a place for refreshment along the way, while the other also provided food, drink and shelter for the weary traveller. Later, inns were set up as private concerns, or were taken over from the religious houses. During the Middle Ages they were

5 The cellarer takes a sly sip of the wine he is drawing to serve the monks and any guests receiving the hospitality of the monastery.

usually situated inside the city walls in order to be safe from robbers when the gates were closed at sunset. For the benefit of the delayed traveller, however, braver people began to build inns against, but on the outside of, the city walls. The doors were kept fastened until a traveller knocked and showed himself to be a genuine customer.

The standard of hospitality in Elizabethan inns is praised by some contemporary writers, who mention the excellent food, wine and beer, the scrupulously clean table cloths and bedlinen, the tapestries on the walls and the advantages of having a key to one's room. But unfortunately the willing servants and the jolly hosts were sometimes in league with highwaymen. The attentive enquiries about the traveller's route and the helpful carrying of luggage might merely be in order to let robbers know whether the guest was likely to have valuables in his bags, and if so which road he was going to take.

Inns also provided a meeting place for the local inhabitants. Often the squire and his guests at the manor-house, after dining at home, would adjourn to the local inn and spend hours in a private room talking and drinking. This was especially likely if the squire had greater confidence in the innkeeper's cellar than in his own. For the poorer people, the inn or ale-house was the only social centre they had.

A Taste for Wine
The Christian Church has always had a great interest in wine, and the great religious orders have made an important contribution to standards of wine.

11

Every monastery had its cellarer whose duty was to provide good, sound wine, not only for sacramental purposes but also for the refreshment of the monks and their guests. Some monasteries also experimented with distillation and with the addition of honey, herbs and flavourings to produce liqueurs. In the early Middle Ages vines were grown fairly widely in England, though it has been claimed that this was a constant struggle against failure, as there was rarely enough sun to ripen the grapes sufficiently to produce good wine. However, the climate was no more unsuitable than that of the north Rhineland vineyards.

In fact the decline of English wine-making can be attributed almost entirely to the marriage in 1152, of Prince Henry of England to Princess Eleanor of Aquitaine. She brought as her dowry to the English Crown all the west of France — Normandy, Brittany, Anjou and Gascony — the chief wine-producing areas of France. A plentiful supply of the best red wine in the world was grown on an estuary within easy sailing distance of England. Thus the infant English wine industry was smothered at birth by its more vigorous and fruitful French mother.

A thriving trade between England and Bordeaux soon developed, and during the next 300 years Bordeaux wine was an everyday English drink. The retail price of wine was 1½p a gallon, while beer was ½p a gallon. The first cargo of Gascon wine came to Southampton in 1213, and to Bristol in the following year. By 1273, 8,846 tuns of wine (equivalent to 10 million bottles today) were imported, and the customs duty charged on it was 2 shillings (10p) a tun. A few years later, 73 ships arrived in London, each having on board 19 tuns of wine, and the Crown claimed of this 'one tun before the mast and one tun behind the mast'. So much of the shipping trade was engaged in the handling of wine casks, each of which occupied 60 cubic feet (approximately 2 cubic metres) in the hold of a ship, that 'tonnage', the number of tuns a ship could carry, became the universally accepted measure of a vessel's capacity, and is still used today.

The wine trade between England and Gascony was of great value, and both sides heavily depended on it. The whole district around Bordeaux concentrated on the cultivation of vines, and Gascony relied on England for its grain, which was exported to France even in times of lean harvest in England. Gascony provided a profitable market for English cloth. Even during the Hundred Years' War (1337-1453), although there was some confusion and shortage of supplies, the trade continued. By the fifteenth century England was importing 3 million gallons (13.6 million litres) of wine a year — one third of the value of her whole import trade.

Wine at this time did not last long, usually not more than a year (partly because sugar was not added to the juice to increase the strength of the wine as is done now, and partly because secure corking was unknown). In 1226 for example, Henry III instructed his cellarer at Bristol 'to sell off the old wine and buy new wine with the proceeds'. The autumn vintage would be more or less undrinkable by the following summer. In fact about three-quarters of the wine drunk in the Middle Ages would be regarded as quite undrinkable today. Peter of Blois, a clerk at Henry II's court, gave this description of the wine often served in the royal household:

> The wine is turned sour or mouldy: thick, greasy, stale, flat and smacking of pitch. I have sometimes seen even great lords served with wine so muddy that a man must needs close his eyes and clench his teeth, wry-mouthed, and filtering the stuff rather than drinking.

One of the popular drinks of this time was *vin cuit* (cooked wine); the wine was

6 Tending a vineyard in France in the fifteenth century. Grapes are being gathered in baskets of a shape still used today, new plants are being staked out and casks collected.

7 Work in the vineyard and the making of wine are shown in a fifteenth-century French manuscript. Note the grapes being pressed by foot in the vat.

boiled down to about one-third of its original volume to make it stronger, and was pepped up with spices. Another favourite was hippocras made from red and white wine, herbs and spices, especially ginger, and strained through a long linen bag called a 'Hippocrates Sleeve' because it was like the sleeves apothecaries wore. Clarry was a sweet wine mixed with honey and spices, while claret (from the French *clairet*) was clear red wine from Bordeaux. There were many other popular drinks in the Middle Ages whose names are quite unknown today — among them Antioche, Bastard, Malespine, Vernage, Pontac, Rochelle, Rumney, Tyre, Caprick, Campolet, Raspice, Osey, Mountross and Ryvere.

A great spate of regulations about the sale of wine date from the thirteenth century. Among the first was a law passed in the reign of King John (1199-1216) which laid down maximum prices for Anjou and Poitou wines. In subsequent reigns many more wines were added to the list. To prevent importers evading the payment of customs duties, Richard III decreed that wine could only be imported in standard butts holding 126 gallons (570 litres). There were also regulations about the quality of wine. In 1363 Edward III granted the Company of Vintners a charter, under which English vintners were allowed to go abroad to buy wine, but foreign merchants were only

14

allowed to sell wine wholesale in England. The charter stated:

> Each year the Mystery of Vintners shall select four most knowledgeable persons from among themselves who shall — not keeping a tavern themselves — inspect all wines sold by other vintners and see that they are reasonably priced, in good condition and correctly named.

This part of the charter was soon invoked to some purpose when, in the following year, John Rightwys and John Penrose were charged with selling 'red wine, unsound and unwholesome for men to the deceit of the common people and shameful disgrace of the officers of the City.' Rightwys was acquitted, but Penrose was sentenced to drink a draught of his own wine and have the rest poured over his head. In 1583 Queen Elizabeth I allowed the Vintners' Company to impose fines on vintners employing anyone who had not served a proper apprenticeship in the guild, and on anyone taking on more apprentices than they could 'honestly guide'.

Drunkenness

Although the picture usually presented in Shakespeare's time is of merry drinking, there was already some concern about the 'beastly vice of drunkenness'. One writer spoke about the abundance of ale-houses, taverns and inns where people sat:

> at the wine and good-ale all day long, yea, all the night too, peradventure a whole week together, so long as any money is left; swilling, gulling and carousing ... till never a one can speak a word ... How they stut and stammer, stagger and reel to and fro like madmen ... swearing, cursing and banning, interlacing their speeches with curious terms of blasphemy.

Philip Stubbes went on to present a horrible picture of a drunken man who resembled a brute rather than a Christian:

> For do not his eyes begin to stare and to be red, fiery and bleared, blubbering forth seas of tears? Doth he not froth and foam at the mouth like a boar? Doth not his tongue falter and stammer in his mouth? Doth not his head seem as heavy as a millstone, he not being able to bear it up ... Is not his understanding altogether decayed? Do not his hands, and all his body vibrate, quaver and shake? ... it weakeneth the natural strength, it corrupteth the blood, it disolveth the whole man at the length, and finally maketh him forgetful of himself altogether, so that what he doth being drunk, he remembereth not being sober. The drunkard in his drunkenness killeth his friend, revileth his lover, discloseth secrets and regardeth no man.

15

3. New Drinking Habits, 1600~1750

In the middle of the seventeenth century three new drinks were introduced into England that were to cause a social revolution — coffee, chocolate and tea. At first tea was very expensive, but within a century it had become the main national beverage. The drinking habits of the whole country changed completely, and a new kind of social meeting place, the coffee house, appeared.

Coffee

Coffee did not reach Europe until the seventeenth century, though it had been known in eastern countries for many centuries. There is a legend that coffee was discovered over a thousand years ago, when an Arab goat-herd found that his goats became frisky and did not sleep after eating the leaves and berries of a particular shrub. An abbot who was told the story steeped some of the berries in water and gave the liquid to his monks to drink. He reported that it kept them awake and reverent instead of falling asleep over their prayers!

It is believed that Ethiopia was the original home of coffee; about the sixth century AD, people there found that chewing coffee beans helped to sustain them on long journeys. Arab slave traders picked up the habit and took the plant home. It seems that the first cultivated coffee plants were grown in the Yemen.

Coffee, which was first eaten as a paste, became especially popular among the Moslems, to whom alcoholic drinks were forbidden by their prophet Mohammed. For a time people were suspicious of this stimulating substitute for wine. However, in 1542, it was declared acceptable to Moslems and its popularity grew. The cultivation of coffee spread round Aden and Medina, and the Moslem pilgrims carried it with them on their journeys to Mecca. Coffee reached Cairo, Syria and Constantinople in the sixteenth century. It became so popular in Constantinople that prayers were neglected, and the religious authorities frowned upon the coffee houses.

After tasting coffee on their travels, European merchants brought it back to their own countries. Oxford claims to be the first place in England where coffee was drunk, and the first place to have a coffee house. In 1652 the first London coffee house was opened, in an alley off Cornhill, by Pasqua Rosée, the servant of an English merchant who had brought back supplies of coffee from Turkey. The coffee house was an immediate success, and soon similar houses were springing up all over town, despite the complaints that they caused a nuisance with their 'evil smells'.

Pasqua Rosée's hand bill advertising his new coffee house described

8 A coffee kiosk looking out on the busy harbour at Constantinople (modern Istanbul), in Turkey. As Moslems are forbidden by their religion to drink alcohol, coffee houses took the place of inns and taverns as social centres.

9 An illustration from a broadsheet advertising coffee in 1676 shows the coffee shrub and its berries and an early coffee house.

the growth of the plant in Arabia and how it is 'dried in an oven and ground into a powder, and boiled up with spring water . . . to be taken as hot as can possibly be endured.' He also explained that 'it will prevent drowsiness, and make one fit for business . . . and therefore you are not to drink it after supper, unless you intend to be watchful, for it will hinder sleep for three or four hours.'

Londoners soon found, as the Moslems had, that the new beverage was a stimulant as well as being pleasant to drink. London coffee houses became centres of social life and greatly influenced the habits of City merchants and other men about town. They were places of relaxation and relief from the exhausting drinking habits of the time, since there was no alcohol allowed on the premises. 'For persons much concerned in the world,' said one writer, coffee houses were superior 'to taverns and ale-houses, where continual sippings, tho' never so warily, would be apt to fly up into their brains and render them drowsy and indisposed for business.' Foreign visitors found the coffee houses attractive places, providing calm, comfortable surroundings at reasonable prices. A French traveller wrote: 'You have a good fire, which you may sit by as long as you please: you have a dish of coffee: you meet your friends for the Transaction of Business, and all for a Penny, if you don't care to spend more.' A German visitor described how he had seen a preacher write his sermon in a coffee house:

In these coffee houses quietness is the rule. If they speak, they speak softly together. Most of them read the papers and nobody disturbs another. The room is entered from the street directly by the front door and the seats are separated by wooden wainscotting. Many letters and proposals are written out: you can often see something in a newspaper dated from a coffee house.

Another account, however, described a noisier place. Ned Ward's book *Secret History of Clubs* talks about Old Man's in Scotland Yard where 'the clashing of their snuff-box lids [in opening and shutting] made more noise than their tongues. Bows and cringes of the newest mode were here exchanged . . . they made a humming like so many hornets in a country chimney.'

By Queen Anne's reign (1702-14) there were nearly 500 coffee houses in London; every respectable Londoner had his favourite one where his friends or clients could seek him out at known hours. The upper classes met at White's, Boodle's and Almack's where there was gambling for high stakes. The Tories went to the Cocoa Tree Chocolate House, the Whigs to St James's Coffee House; poets, critics and their patrons frequented Will's near Covent Garden, scholars went to the Grecian, the clergy to Truby's. The coffee house was a cheap and informal kind of club where men from all walks of life could relax or take part in lively discussion and keep up to date in current affairs. In the days before telegrams and effective journalism, they were centres for political, military and

10 A busy coffee house in Queen Anne's reign. Note the heated argument which has led to the throwing of a bowl of coffee into one of the customers' face.

general news as well as news for commercial purposes. Towards the end of the eighteenth century, stockbrokers deserted the Royal Exchange for the coffee houses, among them Jonathon's and Garraway's. In 1773, because of increased business, the stockbrokers decided that they needed premises of their own and set up the Stock Exchange in Threadneedle Street. They still do business on 'the floor of the House', so named since coffee house days, and the attendants, wearing blue and red uniforms with gold-braided top hats, are still referred to as 'waiters'.

> Coffee which makes the politician wise,
> And see through all things with his half-shut eyes,

wrote Alexander Pope. But for women, who were not allowed in them, the coffee houses were less attractive. The wives of men who frequented the coffee houses complained that their husbands were being lured away from home. Some sent a petition to King Charles II attacking coffee, which they claimed affected their husbands' ability to have children, making them 'as unfruitful as the sandy deserts, from where that unhappy berry is said to be brought.' The 'Women's Petition Against Coffee' argued that coffee, as well as leading to a fall in the birth rate, led to coffee houses being used by men as a refuge in times of domestic crisis when they should have been attending to duties at home. A spirited counter-attack followed in the 'Men's Answer to the Women's Petition'. Charles II was glad to use the women's grievances as an excuse for closing the coffee houses, which he believed were centres of critical talk and possibly sedition. In December 1675, he issued a Royal Proclamation that all coffee houses should be closed within two weeks. But such was the public outcry against this interference with liberty that the order was rescinded. The coffee houses remained centres of London's social and business life for another hundred years.

During the eighteenth century coffee houses were opened beyond the immediate vicinity of the City of London. They too tended to become meeting places for particular arts, professions or political persuasions. Baston's was patronized by doctors, and also by patients seeking medical advice; at the London in Ludgate Hill, property was auctioned, the George in the Strand was popular with the legal profession, and the Chapter in Paternoster Row was a meeting place for booksellers and authors. For the entrance fee of one penny, men could gather in the smoke-laden rooms and listen to the literary and political wisdom of the great men of the day. Tobacco smoke and smoke from the big open fires mingled with the aroma of coffee constantly being roasted and brewed. Dishes of steaming coffee at 1p a time were served to the customers sitting or standing around in gossiping groups. Steele and Addison gathered information for the *Spectator* and the *Tatler* in the coffee houses, which also provided the means of circulation for the newspapers.

11 The importance of the coffee house in contemporary political life is shown in Hogarth's drawing of a Member of Parliament and the journalist Joseph Addison discussing Parliamentary questions in Button's Coffee House.

But as the century wore on coffee houses began to decline. Many of them started to sell alcoholic drinks as well, and they lost their previous relaxed and democratic character. Snobbery led some groups to make their coffee houses exclusive, and turn them into literary or political clubs. The government of the time was glad to see the decline of the coffee houses — like Charles II, they saw them as centres of possible disaffection. Moreover, the British East India Company was importing more and more tea from the Far East, and the government which benefited from the customs duty on tea was anxious to encourage this growing trade. Tea became fashionable at Court and in drawing rooms, and ladies hoped that their menfolk would begin to drink tea at home instead of going out to the coffee houses.

The coffee houses had made a major contribution to the social history of the seventeenth and eighteenth centries. Bach composed a Coffee Cantata; Hogarth and Rowlandson based some of their finest paintings on the life of the coffee houses. The coffee houses saw the emergence of a new and influential class of men, often of moderate means but with lively modern ideas. These middle-class merchants and professional men wished to discuss ideas, not only about trade and business, but also about the role of government, limitation on royal power and the like. They were often keenly interested in art and literature, and wished to be free to express their views in the press and in conversation. The coffee houses provided the meeting places that such men needed. But as many of these men became themselves established figures in politics, commerce and

12 Aztec Indians roasting and preparing cocoa beans. In the foreground is a grinding stone.

literature, the need for the congenial coffee house declined and they began to fade away.

But coffee was not only drunk in coffee houses; it also affected the social habits of the upper classes at home. Along with tea and chocolate, it was drunk at mid-morning or mid-afternoon as an alternative to wine and ale, and so turned these occasions into a social activity for both sexes, rather than a male drinking affair. Breakfast tended to become a lighter meal of coffee or chocolate and rolls taken at a later hour than previously, and this led to dinner and supper becoming later too.

Chocolate

The second new drink of the seventeenth century was chocolate, which was discovered by the Spanish explorers of the New World. The Mayan and Aztec Indians used cocoa beans as a form of currency, and the Aztecs also made a drink from ground roasted cocoa beans whipped up in hot water and flavoured with vanilla and spices. Columbus brought back some cocoa beans to Spain but they were considered valueless. However, Cortez tasted the drink at the court of the Aztec Emperor Montezuma where it was drunk cold, thick and unsweetened. The Spaniards used the cocoa beans Cortez brought back to make a paste of ground beans, sugar, vanilla and cinnamon — the forerunner of our bars of chocolate — which was diluted into a drink. The Spaniards also planted cocoa trees in other parts of their empire, and chocolate later became a favourite drink at the Spanish court, though it was kept as a secret from the rest of Europe for nearly a hundred years.

In 1657 a Frenchman opened a shop in Bishopsgate Street, London, which sold solid chocolate for making a beverage. In England chocolate was drunk hot and with sugar, but at first without milk. Only the wealthy could afford to drink it, but several very fashionable chocolate houses were set up, some of which, White's and St James's for instance, later became gentlemen's clubs. After about 1700 the drink was greatly improved by the addition of milk. High import duties on cocoa beans and block chocolate, however, meant that it remained a luxury item.

Tea

Tea, the third of the new beverages, was first brought to Europe by Dutch traders early in the seventeenth century; it was introduced into England a few years after coffee, and all the early supplies of it came from Holland.

But tea had been well-known in China for centuries. Some legends said that

13 Oliver Goldsmith, Dr Johnson and their circle taking tea at Mrs Thrale's. Dr Johnson said he was 'a hardened and shameless tea drinker'.

the Emperor Shin Nong discovered it 3,000 years before the birth of Christ; others told how in the fifth century AD a Buddhist monk who used to become sleepy while meditating cut off his own eyelids as a punishment and where they fell the first tea plants grew. Whatever its origins, by the seventh and eighth centuries AD the Chinese regarded tea as a stimulant which would keep them awake, and had developed elaborate tea drinking ceremonies.

Tea was first served to the public in England in 1657; it was drunk very weak, with sugar but without milk. It was brewed, kept in a cask, then drawn and warmed up for customers as they asked for it. In spite of this unpromising method of presenting tea, its popularity grew fast. An advertisement for tea appeared in a London newspaper in 1658: 'That Excellent and by all Physicians approved, China drink, called by the Chineans, Tcha, by other Nations Tay or Tee, is sold at the Sultanesshead, a Coffee house in Sweetings Rents by the Royal Exchange, London.' In 1660 Samuel Pepys wrote in his diary: 'Did send for a cup of tea, a China drink which I had never drunk before' and later he commented 'Home, and there find my wife making of Tea.' Charles II's wife, Catherine of Braganza, had already acquired a taste for tea in Portugal and made it fashionable by drinking it at court. In 1664 the East India Company gave Charles II a present of 2lbs 2oz (950 grams) of tea, which they had bought in Holland. However, from 1669 the Company started importing tea direct from China, and in 1721 they were granted a monopoly of tea imports.

When tea first arrived in London it was sold for the enormous price of £3.50 a pound. A few years later, when the East India Company began to bring home supplies, it could be bought for £1 a pound in spite of a heavy tax imposed in 1689. In 1700 imports amounted to about 20,000 lbs (9,000 kg) a year and by the end of the century duty was paid on over 20 million lbs, or about 2 lbs (900 grams) per head of the population. But these official figures make no allowance for the huge quantities of tea that were secretly smuggled into the country.

The government saw in tea an excellent source of revenue. Between 1711 and 1810, £77 million was collected in duties ranging from 12½ to 200 per cent. As a result a flourishing tea smuggling trade grew up. Some of the East India Company's captains were involved, and revenue men were often bribed to keep out of the way when contraband tea was being moved. The coasts of Hampshire, Dorset, Devon and Cornwall were the main centres for this illegal trade with France. Even smuggled tea was expensive; in 1777 the respectable Parson Woodforde paid 10sh 6d (52½p) a lb and a bottle of Geneva (gin) to 'Andrews the smuggler' who brought him 'about 11 o'clock a bag of Hyson Tea 6 pound weight' and frightened him a little 'by whistling under the parlour window' just as he was going to bed. The situation had become so ridiculous that in 1784, the year after he became Prime Minister, William Pitt slashed the import duty on tea to 12½ per cent. Smuggling stopped almost overnight. Pitt's action, however, was too late to save the American colonies. Tea had been introduced into New England almost simultaneously with the mother country, but in America it became an issue to cause a revolution.

England emerged victorious from the Seven Years' War with France (1756-63), though bowed down with a great burden of debt. The war, which had been partly to protect the interests of British colonists in America, had been costly, and Britain tried to compel the colonists to share the load by imposing on them certain taxes. The response was an ominous rumbling of colonial discontent which grew louder as Britain pressed her claims. Resentment grew on both sides. The British tax-payer discovered that he was paying 50 times as much as the American colonist, while the colonists' chief complaint was that they were being taxed by a Parliament that did not represent them. In 1765 the British Parliament passed the Stamp Act whereby tax stamps had to be fixed to such things as newspapers, university degrees and tavern licences. 'Taxation without representation is tyranny' came the colonists' protest. In 1767 taxes were imposed on certain colonial imports including paint, lead, glass and tea. All the duties were repealed in 1770 except the tax on tea which was to be 3d (1½p) per pound. The Americans were very keen on tea, and consumed some 2 million cups a day. To avoid paying the tax the colonists began to drink smuggled Dutch tea and refused to touch the taxed tea shipped by the East India Company. This added to the British financial problems so the government gave the East India Company permission to ship tea direct to America. This cut out the English middleman and caused the price to drop from £1 to 50p a pound, which was cheaper than Dutch smuggled tea.

But the Americans were not appeased. Tea had become a political issue. A vigorous anti-tea campaign was mounted. Colonists were warned that drinking tea would not only destroy their liberty but would make them weak and effeminate. The first three ships carrying tea direct from China arrived in Boston late in 1773. The colonists refused to allow them to unload their cargo while the Governor insisted that tax on the tea should be paid. Tempers flared, and a group of American patriots dressed as Red Indians boarded the ships and threw 342 chests of tea, worth £10,000, into Boston harbour. This 'Boston Tea Party' sparked off the American War of Independence, as a result of which Britain lost her American colonies. In America, from having been the favourite drink, tea became the symbol of oppression and since this time Americans have drunk more coffee than tea.

Back in England the low tax on tea did not last long. By 1793 England was at war again with France, and in order to raise revenue, the tax on tea rose from 25 per cent in 1795 to 96 per cent by 1806.

By the second half of the eighteenth century tea was more popular than coffee or chocolate and was drunk with milk or cream and sugar. It was still something of a luxury and the lady of the household kept her tea in a caddy which she locked after use. There was, however, some opposition to tea on

14 'The Boston Tea Party' — the destruction of the tea cargo which is being thrown into Boston Harbour. Note the Chinese markings on the tea chests.

15 Ranelagh Gardens, Chelsea, was a famous tea garden with a lake which had a Chinese house in the middle of it. The great Rotunda seen in the background had a huge circular room with tiers of boxes to provide cover in cool weather.

grounds of health. The preacher John Wesley claimed that tea-drinking affected his nerves and made his hand shake. He first tried taking it weaker, then with more milk and sugar and finally gave it up altogether. Dependence on tea, he claimed, brought one near to 'the Chamber of Death'.

The great change in drinking habits and the popularity of tea disturbed others beside John Wesley. Some feared that tea would supplant ale and beer, which they considered healthy and natural drinks, and criticised working people who spent so much on luxuries like tea and sugar. One writer estimated that, out of an annual income of £40, it was not unusual for a working class family to spend £2 a year on tea. In the cottages of Middlesex and Surrey, he said, 'tea is not only the usual beverage in the morning and evening, but is generally drunk in large quantities at dinner. Whether this exotic is more palatable or more nutritious than home-raised barley converted into broth, I leave it to Medical Gentlemen to determine.' Men were losing their stature, women their beauty and 'your very Chamber-maids have lost their bloom,' said another critic, 'I suppose by sipping tea ... You may see labourers who are mending the roads drinking their tea ... it is even sold out of cups to haymakers ... were they the sons of tea sippers who won the fields of Crecy and Agincourt or dyed the Danube's shores with Gallic blood?' On the other hand, others believed that tea had medicinal value, and would help to cure scurvy.

As the habit of tea-drinking spread, sugar consumption rose. It was no longer a luxury since trade with the West Indies brought in large supplies of reasonably priced sugar. The popularity of tea caused a sharp decline in the sale of coffee, cocoa and chocolate, all of which were much more expensive than tea. Towards the end of the eighteenth century many of the once famous coffee houses had disappeared.

During this time the public pleasure gardens of London — such as Vauxhall, Marylebone, Cuper's and Ranelagh — some of which had been none too respectable, transformed themselves into tea gardens and became very popular. They had a season from May to early autumn and although all kinds of drink were available, including coffee and chocolate, tea was the most fashionable drink. Admission to the gardens cost one shilling (5p) and refreshments were extra, but at Ranelagh the charge was half-a-crown (12½p) which included tea or coffee, and bread and butter. Some of the gardens had concerts, dancing and bowling greens, but most of the pleasure was derived from walking around and meeting friends, and drinking tea together in the open air.

The vogue for afternoon tea became established in the second half of the eighteenth century. The Duchess of Bedford started the habit as she ate a huge breakfast, had little lunch but used to suffer from what she called 'a sinking feeling' around five o'clock. She therefore ordered tea and cakes to be served in the afternoon and this feminine ritual remained until quite recent times.

4. The Rise of Spirit Drinking

Spirits were known in Britain in Tudor times but they were not widely drunk. By the beginning of the seventeenth century, however, attitudes had changed, and there are frequent references in contemporary writing to aquavitae, which was a distilled spirit like a crude gin. Aquavitae was distilled from fermented grain or such things as fruit, wine dregs and old cider. Queen Elizabeth had granted a monopoly to prepare aquavitae to Richard Drake as a reward for his services under Sir Francis Drake, but this lapsed after 1601. By 1621, when a petition was presented to Parliament for the protection of distillers and sellers of aquavitae and 'other strong and hott waters', there were 200 establishments distilling spirits in the cities of London and Westminster. In 1638 a patent for distilling 'strong waters' was granted to Sir Theodore Mayerne and Thomas Cadman. They founded the Distillers' Company in the same year. Rules and regulations were drawn up about methods and standards of distilling. In 1690, when the patent lapsed, an Act of Parliament laid down the standards for 'good and wholesome brandies, aquavitae and spirits, drawn and made from malted corn'. This use of the word brandy for spirits distilled from materials other than wine was a measure directed against the French, the main producers of brandy. The spirit was like a raw, crude whisky or schnapps, and was sometimes known as 'British brandy'.

The Demon Gin

Early in the eighteenth century English farmers were having difficulty in selling all their grain, so the government, which represented the interests of landowners, decided to help them by encouraging the distilling of gin from grain. They cancelled the tax on distilling, abolished control of manufacturing standards, and allowed gin to be sold without a licence. The government hoped that these measures would bring greater prosperity to the farmers and destroy the trade in smuggled French brandy. Distilling consumed a great deal of corn, which was good for the landowners, but it was to have appalling social consequences.

The word 'gin' is short for 'Geneva', and originates from the Dutch word *genever* (or the French *genievre*) for the juniper berries that were used to flavour the drink. English soldiers probably drank it in the Low Countries at the end of the sixteenth century. It was very strong, rough stuff and was sometimes drunk before going into battle, to give the soldiers 'Dutch courage'. Gin became widely drunk in England after the Dutch King William III came to the throne in 1689.

16 A caricaturist's impression of human nature giving way to excess in food, drink and behaviour.

The British public responded enthusiastically to the government's invitation to drink more gin. The consumption of gin on which excise duty (only 2d [1p] a gallon) had been paid, rose from half a million gallons in 1700 to more than five million in 1735; and it is impossible to know how much more illicit gin, on which no duty was paid, was produced and consumed. Gin was drunk throughout the country, though it seems that ale held its own better in the villages than in the towns. London was, however, the greatest sufferer from the gin-drinking epidemic.

Gin shops sprang up in every nook and cranny. Gin was made out of any substance which would ferment, and could be bought in thousands of 'dives' and cellars in back streets and alleys. In slum areas like St Giles in London, every fourth or fifth house sold 'gin'. A publican in Southwark put up a notice which read: 'Drunk for 1d. Dead drunk for 2d. Clean straw for nothing.' Everyone sold gin. A contemporary report declared that dram-sellers 'sell even in the streets and highways, some on bulks set up for that purpose and others in wheelbarrows, and many more who sell privately in garrets, cellars, backrooms and other places . . . All chandlers, many tobacconists and such who sell fruit and herbs in stalls . . . sell geneva, and many inferior tradesmen begin now to keep it in their shops for their customers.' Some employers sold gin to their workers, 'on the slate', which meant that the workers were always in debt and owed a good part of their wages before they even earned them. The annual consumption of spirits in London at this time was 14 gallons (63 litres) a head, and the average Londoner also drank 90 gallons (400 litres) of beer.

While the epidemic of the 'great destroyer' lasted, and it reached its peak between 1720 and 1750, the health of the nation was seriously affected. Hogarth's famous 'Gin Lane' sets out clearly the horrors of a gin-sodden society with the inevitable pawn-shop, violence, ill-health, debauchery and neglect of children. He contrasted this with the prosperous 'Beer Street'. Gin-drinking caused thousands of deaths, and many of the poor became so dependent on it 'that they will suffer any punishment,' said a report, 'rather than live without it.' Some addicts would pawn all their possessions to obtain money for their next gin, and then might turn to robbery or murder to pay for more drinks. Women gave gin to babies-in-arms to make them sleep more soundly, which contributed no doubt to the terrifyingly high infant death rate. During the early years of the eighteenth century, the death rate was greater than the birth rate; it is believed that the growth of gin-drinking was a major cause of this. At the height of the gin-drinking craze, between 1740 and 1742, there were twice as many burials in London as christenings; and during the 30-year period when gin-drinking was uncontrolled the population of London was drastically reduced.

Although drinkers, sellers and distillers of gin were all opposed to reform,

17 Hogarth's 'Gin Lane' provided vivid propaganda about the results of the cheap gin policy. He contrasted this with his 'Beer Street' which showed the healthier and more prosperous results of beer-drinking.

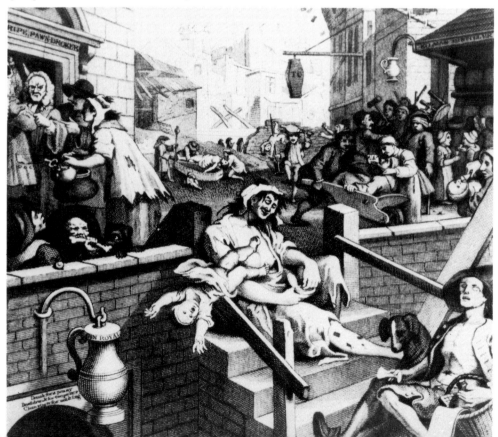

the government began to be concerned about the effect gin was having on public health. In 1736 the Gin Act fixed a licence fee of £50 for gin sellers, prohibited the sale of gin in quantities of less than two gallons (9 litres) and put a tax of £1 a gallon on it. They wanted to make gin too expensive for the poor, and the measures consequently provoked some rioting and disorder. However, it was soon clear that the Act could be easily evaded and in no time the brandy shops in London were selling tots of 'Sangaree', 'Tow-row', 'Bob', 'Ladies Delight', 'Cuckold's Comfort', 'King Theodore of Corsica' or 'Grape Waters' without mentioning the word gin. Chemists' shops sold gin in medicine bottles as a cure for various ills. In the first two years after the passing of the Act, 12,000 people were convicted for offences against it. The only people who liked the Act were those who made a handsome living out of denouncing illegal gin shops.

One enterprising man hit on a good way to make money. He nailed a sign of a cat to the ground floor window of his house and under the paw of the cat he fixed a lead pipe with a funnel at the end. Passers-by were invited to put their money in the cat's mouth and whisper, 'pussy give me two pennoth of gin', when a tot would come gushing through the funnel. This was surely a very early version of a coin-in-the-slot machine and is said to have made its inventor

18 'The Drunkard's Progress' of steady decline is traced from the Pawnbroker's shop to the Gin Shop, then on to the Workhouse, to Prison and finally to be hanged at the Scaffold.

an excellent profit.

The gin-sellers were active even in the gaols. Conditions of health and hygiene in eighteenth-century prisons were appalling but anyone whose friends had money could have food and drink supplied by the gaolers, who made a handsome profit out of it. Gin was one of the most popular items to be sold. A report on the gaols of the City of London, Westminster and Southwark in 1776 stated that 'upwards of 120 gallons [540 litres] of gin, which they call by various names, such as vinegar, gossip, crank, Mexico, skyblue etc, were sold weekly, besides other spirits in proportion. The beer consumed amounts, by calculation, to eight butts a week', though later 24 butts a week were drunk.

It had been expected that the 1736 Act would curb gin-drinking and injure the prosperity of the farmers. A contemporary song mourned:

> Good luck, good luck and well-a-day
> That Madam Gin should fall;
> Superior power one must obey
> This Act will starve us all.

But the Act soon proved a complete failure and sales of gin even increased. In 1742 the Act was replaced since it could not be enforced and was making the law an object of contempt and ridicule. 'It was such a law as could not be executed', said a member of the House of Lords, but 'the poor had run gin-mad, the rich had run anti-gin-mad, and in this fit of madness no-one would give ear to reason.'

By the middle of the eighteenth century the situation was causing great concern not only in London but also in other towns such as Bristol, Salisbury, Rochester, Manchester and Norwich, where increasing lawlessness and idleness led to petitions being sent to Parliament. In his 'Report into the Causes of the late Increase of Robbers', Henry Fielding, magistrate and novelist, wrote about drunkenness caused by:

> The strongest intoxicating liquors, and particularly that poison called gin, which I have reason to believe is the principal sustenance (if it may be so called) of more than a hundred thousand people in this metropolis. Many of these wretches there are who swallow pints of this poison within the twenty-four hours; the dreadful effects of which I have the misfortune every day to see, and smell too.

At last the authorities decided to take drastic measures. In 1751 a very heavy tax was put on spirits, and severe penalties were imposed on illegal distilling. Strict limitations on the retail sale of gin were also made. Some riots followed these drastic measures and mock funerals for 'Madame Gin' were held, with the mourners getting suitably drunk to drown their sorrows. The tax on gin was raised again in 1756 and for a time the distillation of gin from corn was prohibited because of bad harvests. By 1760 the tax on gin had reached the very high figure of £24.50 a tun. This was because the government had begun to realize that, under the guise of discouraging excessive drinking, they could add considerably to the national revenue. In addition, the sharp rise in the price of grain brought a great reduction in the distilling of spirits from grain, since it had ceased to be a cheap process. Gin was no longer the drink of the poor; the public was forced to turn to beer and other cheaper and healthier drinks. By the end of the century, instead of the British public tippling about eight million gallons of gin every year, the amount consumed had dropped to about one million gallons.

19 George Cruikshank's very condemnatory impression of a gin shop and the death and misery it caused. He was an active supporter of the temperance movement.

In contrast to the beer trade which was held in public favour, there tended to be a stigma about being engaged in the gin trade. Some of the famous distillers, such as Booths, were established in the eighteenth century and, though they made fortunes, they were never as acceptable in society as the beer-brewing families and were never awarded peerages.

Whisky and Rum
Although excessive whisky-drinking can have just as serious effects on health

20 In contrast to the sordid gin shops an eighteenth-century ale-house is shown as clean, orderly and respectable.

and social life, it has never been viewed as critically as gin. Gin is of comparatively recent origin, but whisky has a long history dating back to ancient times. The name whisky comes from the Celtic word *uisge-beatha* 'the water of life'. The most famous whisky is 'Scotch', though like the bagpipes and Christianity, it may have come first from Ireland. Its distinctive flavour derives from home-grown barley, water from Scottish burns, and inherited skill in its preparation.

By the seventeenth century whisky was as essential a part of the Scotsman's diet as porridge. The simplest home had a bottle of whisky to give a drink of what Robert Burns called 'poor man's wine' to any caller. In 1660 a duty of twopence (1p) a gallon was put on whisky, but it was unenforceable and generally ignored. After the massacre at Culloden (1746) the clan system in Scotland was broken up and the wearing of tartans and carrying of arms was forbidden; excise-men also tried to enforce the whisky taxes and get rid of illegal stills, but they were persistently outwitted. 'The ruddy complexion, nimbleness and strength of these people is not owing to water-drinking', said one excise man, 'but to the aquavitae, a malt spirit which serves for both victual and drink'. The Scots also smuggled whisky across the Border to meet a growing demand from the English who wanted to avoid the import duty.

21 'The Highland Still' by Sir David Wilkie. Illegal stills in Scotland were easily concealed from the excise-men.

Scotch remained a drink mainly for home consumption until well into the nineteenth century. It was largely made in farmhouse stills, and was usually of high quality, but it is difficult to estimate how much of it was drunk. However, by the nineteenth century, the illegal stills were disappearing and most whisky was subject to duty. A comparison of spirit drinking at this time, in England, Ireland and Scotland, based on duty paid, shows that in England the rate was almost half a gallon per person per year, in Ireland it was nearly two-thirds of a gallon, but in Scotland they drank more than two gallons for every man, woman and child. And it seems probable that much more untaxed whisky was also drunk. The Highlander drank whisky for his breakfast and throughout the day, but he lived in healthy surroundings, took regular exercise and ate unadulterated food, whereas the gin-drinker in English towns lived in insanitary, overcrowded conditions, and ate unwholesome food. When the Scottish industrial centres began to grow, creating similar slum conditions to those in England, the problem of strong drink became just as serious, and whisky just as dangerous an enemy as gin.

Another spirit that became popular during the eighteenth century was rum which was imported in large quantities from the West Indies. Rum is a spirit made from pure cane sugar or from molasses, which is the treacly residue after

35

sugar crystals have been crushed from the sugar cane. Rum (originally called tafia) was first exported to Europe by Portuguese settlers in Brazil in the sixteenth century. After Columbus had discovered the West Indian islands in 1492, the Spaniards introduced the cultivation of the sugar cane to the area and it has remained an important crop ever since. By the early seventeenth century, a drink called 'Kill Devil' or 'rumbullion' was being made in Barbados, and this was later known as rum. Versions of this drink were soon being produced all round the Caribbean. Until fairly recently it was considered rather a 'low' drink, suitable only for sailors. In 1731 sailors in the Navy were given the choice of a daily pint of wine or half-a-pint of rum instead of their ration of beer (a gallon a day!). In 1740 Admiral Vernon, nicknamed 'old grog' because of his coat which was made of grogram (a coarse fabric of silk and wool mixture), ordered that the rum ration to sailors should be diluted with water, and this mixture became known as grog. It must have been a blow to hardened mariners in 1824, when tea was introduced into the Navy and the rum ration was cut to a quarter of a pint.

Wine, Madeira and Port

In the seventeenth century large quantities of French wines were drunk by the middle and upper classes, both with and after their meals. Samuel Pepys recorded that he had vowed not to drink wine and so was drinking hippocras (made from wine, sugar or honey and spices)! A popular drink was negus named after a Colonel Negus who had commanded a regiment under the Duke of Marlborough and later became a Member of Parliament; when tempers were roused he produced his soothing brew of wine, hot water and sugar. Dr Johnson and Boswell drank a bottle of negus each every night, and split a third bottle between them. Later port was usually used for making negus.

During Marlborough's wars against the French (1702-09), French wines were hard to obtain though they did not disappear entirely from the table — some wine was captured at sea and some was smuggled into the country. However, wines from other sources naturally became more popular, especially from Portugal. The marriage of the Portuguese Princess, Catherine of Braganza, to King Charles II, started a new vogue for drinking Madeira wine. This was a wine, fortified with brandy, from the Portuguese island of Madeira. Catherine introduced the wine to the English Court and started the fashion of drinking it in the mornings with a slice of Madeira cake, a pleasant mid-morning refreshment for ladies which lasted up to Victorian times. But even more popular was another fortified wine, port, called after the town of Oporto in Portugal from where it was shipped. In 1703 the Methuen Treaty gave specially favourable terms to Portuguese traders as opposed to their French competitors; for instance the duty on Portuguese wine was only £7 a tun, whereas the French had to pay £55. In return for low duties on Portuguese wines, English cloth paid only a low duty in Portugal. As a result a Whig who supported this foreign policy had every excuse for drinking three or four bottles of port or Madeira in an evening, though the price of his patriotism might be a severe attack of gout. Jacobites who admired the French drank claret which was not as strong and was less taxing on their digestion. Another drink made fashionable by royal approval was champagne — Charles II returned from his exile in France with a taste for it, but it was expensive and only drunk in privileged circles.

The Cork

At the beginning of the eighteenth century a great invention, the cork, transformed the quality of wine. Before, wine had been kept in barrels until it was wanted when it was drawn off into a decanter or bottle made of leather, earthenware or glass. There could be no question of wine improving or maturing in the bottle or cask; it was in fact steadily deteriorating, and between one vintage and the next might turn into vinegar. Wines with the most sugar in them kept best. But now the cork (and corkscrew which rammed the cork home) provided the perfect method of not-quite-airtight sealing. Long ageing of good wines in the bottle now produced wines of high quality and individual character. The shape of the bottle changed too, from the old decanter shape which could only stand upright to the modern cylindrical shape which is stored lying down. If a corked bottle is left standing up the cork eventually dries out, shrinks and lets the air in, which turns the wine to vinegar. If the bottle is lying down, the wine touches the cork and prevents it from shrinking.

5. Clean Water to Drink

Early Water Supplies

Man cannot exist without water; he can survive without food for several weeks but can only last without water for a few days. This is because the normal functioning of the body involves a continual loss of water and, since the body cannot store water, the loss must be balanced by a continual supply. Water in fact amounts to between 65 and 70 per cent of an adult's weight. The average adult needs to take in about five pints (2.8 litres) of water every day, and he gets this from his solid foods, many of which contain a high proportion of water, as well as from the liquids he drinks. Normally he expels about five pints of water a day through the lungs, the skin, the intestines and the kidneys.

Early man had to live near to some natural source of water supply — a spring, a stream or a lake. Stone Age Man learned how to reach supplies of underground water by digging wells, and some of these reached a considerable depth. These wells had to be dug by hand and could only be made where the soil was suitable; it was not until iron tools were in use that long tunnels and aqueducts could be built. Then towns no longer had to depend on local supplies. Even in the ancient world water was conveyed to towns over considerable distances.

The Romans laid great emphasis on water supply, and there were no water engineers as expert as them for nearly a thousand years. The Romans brought supplies from the mountains to be stored in reservoirs and cisterns in cities, with numerous outlets to public fountains and baths. Some of the richer Romans had water directly connected to their homes. It is estimated that the daily consumption of water per head in Rome was 50 gallons (227 litres), which is not much lower than that of many modern cities today.

The Middle Ages and After

During the Dark Ages most of the Roman waterworks fell into ruin, and cities began once again to rely upon local springs, wells and rivers. The Normans made sure of a water supply before building a castle; the well was always in the keep so that they would not lack water in case of siege. Sometimes monasteries took the responsibility for maintaining supplies of fresh water for their own benefit and for that of the surrounding neighbourhood. Supplies in towns were often insufficient and dangerously polluted, and all water had to be drawn by hand.

In London, conduits (water channels) were built in the thirteenth century; the first ran from Tyburn to Cheapside, where it ended in a fountain. Water

22 (*Above*) The Pont du Gard was built by the Romans in about 19 BC to carry fresh water from the hills to the citizens of Nîmes in southern France.

23 (*Below right*) A water-carrier crying 'New River Water' and carrying supplies for sale to people's houses.

was either pumped by hand from shallow wells or led off into fountains in the streets from which it could be carried away in buckets. The poor drew water for themselves, the rich had it carried to their homes for them. In the late fifteenth century it is recorded that 'it was the custom of all apprentices to carry water tankards to serve their masters' houses with water fetched from the Thames or the common conduits.' There were also water-carriers who earned a living by carrying supplies to houses at perhaps a half-penny a pail. The water-carriers became a large and influential body and formed a guild called 'The Brotherhood of Saint Christofer of the Water Carriers'. Drinking water was, however, a dangerous habit. Andrew Boorde, Bishop of Chichester in the early sixteenth century, declared it 'not wholesome, bad for Englishmen, cold, slow, slack of digestion'.

Expanding trade and industry and the growth of towns brought new problems of water supply, and there were many schemes to replace the public water conduits. Sir Francis Drake, for instance, helped to promote a plan to bring water from Dartmoor to Plymouth in 1585. In London several unsuccessful attempts were made to pump water out of the Thames by horse-driven machines, but in 1582, Peter Morice, a Dutchman, was granted a 500-year lease to erect a water-wheel harnessed to a pump at one of the arches of London Bridge. This pump forced the water up into a reservoir from which it was brought to some houses in lead pipes. The water must have been filthy since the incoming tide would bring up garbage from the ships in the pool below the bridge, and the outgoing tide carried sewage. However, a London

Bridge waterworks continued to supply water until the old bridge was pulled down in the 1830s. Shares in Peter Morice's company were then transferred to the New River Company founded by Sir Hugh Myddleton early in the seventeenth century.

Sir Hugh Myddleton's scheme was to tap pure water from springs discovered near Hertford, 20 miles (32 km) out of London. The source was high enough up for the water to run down by force of gravity in an open channel known as the 'New River' for a distance of 38 miles (61 km) to a circular reservoir at Islington. Water of good quality was piped from the reservoir to local houses, and Sir Hugh Myddleton was highly respected as a local benefactor.

A Swiss visiting England during the reigns of George I (1714-27) and George II (1727-60) wrote enthusiastically about the abundant water supply from the 'big reservoir near Islington and that of the [London] Bridge', which carried water by wooden and lead pipes into all the houses. Each private person could pay to have one or two fountains in their houses and poor people who could not afford to pay could get water in many streets, pumps and wells. But Monsieur De Saussure was astonished that it was so little appreciated:

> Would you believe it, though water is to be obtained in abundance . . . none of it is drunk? In this country nothing but beer is drunk . . . It is said that more grain is consumed in England for making beer than for making bread.

Spas

From very early times there were wells and springs which were believed to have specially beneficial properties. Sometimes they were holy wells which had been consecrated and to which pilgrims travelled for purification; at other times they

40

24 (*Opposite*) A view of the King and Queen's Baths, including the Great Pump Room, at Bath. Drinking the water and bathing in it were both believed to be good for the health.

were just places where people gathered to fetch water and exchange gossip. Many later spas were descendants of the ancient holy wells where it was believed that medical cures could be obtained for various complaints by drinking or bathing in the water. The spas often had hot springs containing minerals such as chalybeate, iron and radium and they became resorts for invalids and fashionable holiday centres. Spa, a town in Belgium, was the first of Europe's well-known watering places.

In the sixteenth century Buxton in Derbyshire had become a fashionable resort for 'great numbers of nobility and gentry' who came to drink its water, and were housed in fine lodgings erected by the Earl of Shrewsbury to develop the place. Harrogate, Cheltenham, Leamington and Tunbridge Wells were also frequented, but during the eighteenth century, under the influence of Beau Nash, Bath became the most successful of the English spas. Doing 'the Season' at Bath was primarily a social affair, but drinking the waters in the Pump Room after breakfast was one of the events of the day. Spas were most popular during the eighteenth and early nineteenth centuries; later seaside resorts began to take their place, though those who seriously wanted 'to take the cure' continued to patronize some of the spas. Under medical supervision a visit to a spa to take the waters was often combined with diet and exercise to offset the effects of over-eating and excessive drinking which were common contemporary health hazards.

The Industrial Revolution

The problem of water supply became much more acute after the Industrial Revolution had led to the rapid growth of towns. Water was distributed in pipes made of hollow elm trunks which leaked so badly that it could only be supplied at low pressure and could not be carried to an upstairs cistern. However, as the iron industry developed in the early nineteenth century, iron water mains came into use. At first these pipes could not expand or contract, so they often broke and leaked as badly as the wooden trunks. Later expansion joints were used and water could then be supplied under pressure to cisterns in the upper parts of houses. This not only gave some houses a continual water supply but also made it possible to install water closets. As only a small quantity of water was available, water mains were only turned on for a short time each day during which cisterns in houses were filled up, and people who had no cisterns filled up their containers from standpipes in the streets. The Londoner was, however, comparatively fortunate in having generally some source of water fairly near at hand. Country cottages often had neither a piped supply of water nor a well, and people were forced to gather rainwater in tubs or take most of their water from the nearest ditch.

Although there was an increased supply of water in London in the 1840s, it did little to improve London's health. The 'poisonous' Thames water pumped into the homes was a serious health hazard. The improved water-closet invented by Joseph Bramah may have seemed a great advance, but it created the need to dispose of many gallons of diluted sewage instead of the previous much smaller amount of concentrated excreta. Some of the WCs were connected to sewers, and some to the cesspools with which London was honeycombed. The stench of the River Thames was dreadful, and water companies were forced to take water from higher up the river, where there was only mild pollution from the sewers of Oxford, Henley, Reading and Maidenhead. Houses in prosperous areas were fairly well served, but south of the Thames they were supplied by companies who drew their water from lower down the river, into which 237 public sewers had been emptied. A pamphlet in 1827 declared that 7,000 families in Westminster were supplied with water 'in a state Offensive to the Sight, Disgusting to the Imagination and Destructive to the Health'. A Royal Commission which investigated the sanitary condition of the Thames in 1828 recommended that intakes for water supplies should be moved upstream and that 'suspended matter' should be removed. These recommendations were made for aesthetic and not for health reasons, but public health incidentally benefited. In 1829 James Simpson, who was engineer to the Chelsea Water Company, put his first slow sand filter to work, thus beginning the effective filtering of water supplies which eventually led to the virtual disappearance of water-borne disease in Britain. However, progress was fairly slow — by 1850, only three of the water companies filtered their water and their reservoirs were in any case uncovered.

The connection between sanitation and water supply, and the cholera epidemics of 1831-32, 1849, 1853-54 and 1856 was by no means obvious to the Victorians. Dr John Snow, though treated at first with ridicule, was able to prove that, during an outbreak of cholera in the Soho district of London, the disease was confined to people using a particular pump which had been polluted with sewage from an adjoining cesspool infected by a cholera victim. He also pointed out that Lambeth and Chelsea had similar records for cholera until the Lambeth Water Company moved its intakes up the river above the highest point of sewage discharge — the incidence of cholera among Lambeth water users fell immediately to about 7 per cent of that of the Chelsea Company users.

Edwin Chadwick was an untiring campaigner for adequate drains and water supply; he was involved in many investigations and reports on sanitary conditions, and has been called the father of modern sanitary science. Chadwick, Dr Southwood Smith and Dr John Simon exposed the dangers to health of inadequate sewers and water supplies, and in 1858 it was agreed to

25 Queueing for water at a standpipe in the streets of Bethnal Green, London. Board of Health investigations in 1850 showed that 70,000 London houses were supplied in groups of 20 or 30 by such standpipes, which were only turned on for an hour a day, three days a week.

26 A grim cartoon about the hazards of water-borne diseases carried by the River Thames.

27 The New River Head Works reservoir and filter beds, 1856.

raise £3 million to construct proper drains for London. The 'cleaning-up' of London took place between 1860 and 1870 as a result of public pressure following the discoveries of Pasteur about bacteria and of Lister about the connection between dirt and infection. The new main sewers were finished in 1865, and open sewers and cesspools were filled in by 1870. Towns in the provinces were, however, less advanced than London.

It has been said that sewers are the veins of a town but that water pipes are its arteries, which means that a town can only use as much water as its sewers can take away. When the London sewers were placed under a single Metropolitan Commission of Sewers there were still eight private profit-making water companies. Efforts to get them to unite met with fierce opposition. An Act of 1852 allowed the companies to remain separate but instructed them not to draw water from the Thames below Teddington Lock, and to cover their reservoirs and filter their water. Another cholera outbreak in 1866 caused further alarm, and towns further up the Thames were forbidden to discharge unfiltered sewage into the Thames. By 1870 the quality of London water was quite good and it was mostly on continuous supply. Often, however, there was only a single tap for a whole tenement house. The use of water was steadily increasing; in 1844 seven gallons (32 litres) per person per day was consumed; in 1893 the figure had risen to 31 gallons (140 litres). In 1972-73 the figure for London was 67 gallons (305 litres) each per day (nb the Romans used 50 gallons). The figures, of course, include industrial as well as domestic use.

At the beginning of the nineteenth century the average expectation of life was only 30 years. It was not realized for a long time that a major reason for this low figure was the spread of several water-borne diseases such as cholera, dysentery, typhoid, jaundice and gastro-enteritis, through bad sanitation and infected water. Fortunately people at this time were not great drinkers of water. In 1836 76 gallons (350 litres) of beer were brewed for each inhabitant in London (including children), which amounted to a daily allowance of more than a pint and a half. And tea was now the most popular drink for all classes. In both these drinks the boiling of the water killed some of the germs.

There is no doubt that the improvements in water supply and sanitation led to a fall in the London death rate. The rate stood at about 24 per 1,000 for the years 1847 to 1871; by the latter date a reasonably good water and sewage system had been completed, and in 1873 the figure was 22.5 per 1,000; in the last ten years of the century it had fallen to 19.2. This amounted to a saving of 20,000 lives in London every year.

Before the end of the century other cities were being forced to look farther afield for water supplies. Many began to construct dams to collect water in suitable mountain valleys and then to convey it by pipeline over considerable distances. The technique of constructing such dams with a core of puddled clay had been developed by the great canal engineers in the eighteenth century, who had to provide reservoirs to maintain water levels in their canals. But after a disaster near Sheffield in 1864 when a dam collapsed and 250 lives were lost, future dams were built of masonry. The first and most notable of these masonry dams was built at Vyrnwy in Wales in 1881 to supply Liverpool. It was 144 feet high and a fifth of a mile long and created the largest artificial lake in Europe, containing 12,000 million gallons of water — a great achievement of Victorian engineering. Four years later Manchester carried water through 95 miles (153 km) of tunnel and pipelines from Thirlmere in the Lake District, while in 1893 Birmingham began a water scheme which brought supplies to the city from a chain of reservoirs 74 miles (119 km) away in Wales.

6. Non-Alcoholic Drinks, 1800~1900

Milk

Until the nineteenth century milk was considered more as a source of butter and cheese than as a drink in itself, though large quantities of whey and buttermilk were drunk. One reason for this was that unless milk could be obtained quite fresh from the cow it went sour very quickly. There was also doubt about whether milk was good for health — a most reasonable doubt since we now know that most of the milk sold in towns must have been very dirty, and that milk-borne infection was a serious hazard. It was, however, believed that milk was essential for feeding infants, and where possible wet nurses were used for breast feeding if the mother's milk was not available. Where a woman's milk could not be provided, ass's milk was preferred to cow's milk. Milch-asses were walked around from door to door so that their milk could be drawn directly into the customer's jugs for the use of infants or invalids.

Men learned to domesticate the cow over 6,000 years ago, and to keep it for regular milk supply as well as for its meat. At the time of the ancient Britons there were herds of white cattle in Britain and stories of sacrifices of white bulls. The various invaders of Britain — Celts, Romans, Angles, Saxons, Danes and Normans — brought with them their own breeds of cattle. Under the open-field system of farming, however, there could be no selective stock-breeding, and there was little chance to improve cattle breeds until the eighteenth century when enclosure of the land and the production of more winter fodder led to great advances in scientific cattle breeding. Emphasis at first was on meat production, but by 1875 work was being done on breeds that had a high milk yield.

The milk of the seventeenth and eighteenth centuries was horrifyingly bad. Some of it came from farms on the outskirts of the towns and was brought by milkwomen who walked long distances with a pair of churns on a shoulder yolk crying, 'Milkmaids below'. Most of it came from cows kept in hovels in the back streets, standing ankle-deep in filth and fed on hay and brewers' grains. The milk must have been almost sour as well as dirty by the time it reached the customer, but fortunately it was mostly used for cooking rather than drinking. Milk was fairly cheap at the beginning of the eighteenth century but during the next hundred years its price rose fourfold.

Tobias Smollett's description of London milk in *Humphrey Clinker* (1771) is appalling and convincing:

The milk . . . lowered with hot water, frothed with bruised snails; carried through the streets in open pails, exposed to foul rinsings, discharged from doors and windows, spittle, snot and tobacco quids, from foot-passengers, overflowings from mud-carts, spatterings from coach wheels, dirt and trash chucked into it by roguish boys for the joke's sake, the spewings of infants, who have slabbered in the tin measure which is thrown back in that condition among the milk . . . and finally, the vermin that drops from the rags of the nasty drab that [sells] this precious mixture, under the respectable denomination of milkmaid.

The unhygienic conditions of London's milk supply, and that of other large towns, did not improve until the second half of the nineteenth century. A description of cowsheds in Golden Square, London, in 1847 caused some concern:

Forty cows are kept in them, two in each seven feet of space. There is no ventilation, save by the unceiled tile roof, through which the ammoniacal vapours escape . . . there is at one end a large tank for grains, a store place for turnips and hay, and between them a large receptacle into which the liquid manure drains, and the solid is heaped . . . the stench thence arising [is] unsufferable.

28 (*Below left*) A fifteenth-century woodcut of a cow being milked.

29 (*Below right*) Milkmaids carrying pails of milk on a wooden yoke and ladling it out in very unhygienic conditions in the streets.

30 Cows behind a dairy in Golden Lane, London. They were kept permanently tethered in filthy sheds. The customers brought their own jugs to be filled.

Distribution of the milk was also unwholesome. Pails were 'slung from the yoke of a grubby roundsman puffing a foul clay pipe, flung on a dray, or piled on the floats ... or "prams" ... rarely far from the rear end of a horse and always exposed to a germ-laden air.' And the Victorian housewife would test the freshness of the milk 'by sticking her finger into the pail to see if it was still warm from the cow.'

But by the 1850s the development of railways made it possible to bring country milk up to the towns by train. Milk was first sent by rail to Manchester in 1844, and to London shortly after. During 1854 the Eastern Counties Railway Company alone carried over three million quarts (3.5 million litres) of milk. The railways cut down on costs as well as time, so the milk now available was both fresher and cheaper.

In 1863 cattle plague attacked numbers of cows in Britain and by 1865-67 had reached epidemic proportions, with huge losses of life. The death rate was especially high in the overcrowded, unhygienic city cowhouses. Of 9,531 cows in the area of the Metropolitan Board of Works in London, 5,357 were attacked by the plague and of these only 375 recovered. The lesson was painfully learned; strict sanitary regulations were laid down and as a result most town dairies closed and supplies came almost entirely from the country. By

31 The French scientist, Louis Pasteur (1822-95), working in his laboratory.

1866 two million gallons (9 million litres) were arriving in London each year by rail. Special milk trains began to run, water-coolers were provided at or near the farms, and large churns of tinned steel-plate were used to carry the milk from the trains to the roundsmen. By 1900 milk bottles were beginning to appear but only for milk which had been 'pasteurized' against tuberculosis.

The work of Louis Pasteur, who proved that minute organisms which cause disease are also responsible for fermentation and putrefaction, did not affect the handling of milk until almost the end of the nineteenth century. Pasteur showed that the minute bacteria could be destroyed when fluids are heated to a temperature of about 63°C. This process known as 'pasteurization' was used first to prevent beer and wine from turning bad and, from about 1890, to prevent milk from going sour rather than to kill germs likely to harm the consumer. However, it was soon clear that pasteurization also provided a valuable protection against milk-borne disease. Most of the early pasteurization plants were primitive, with inadequate control of temperature, and the milk was often under- or over-heated and had a 'cooked' taste.

The need to kill the germs in milk was not appreciated for some time. It was argued, for instance, by those who were concerned about serious malnutrition and stunted growth among poor children, that cheaper milk should be supplied to them. A doctor experimented by giving milk at breakfast and supper to factory children aged 12 to 14 who had previously drunk coffee or tea; the children grew four times as fast which, he said, 'proves incontestably that milk is essential to the healthy nutrition of the young'. But the milk sold in towns was often contaminated with germs and a source of infection and epidemics. Serious outbreaks of typhoid and dysentery were caused by infected milk, as well as tubercular glands and joints. An increased consumption of unheated milk would, therefore, have led to more disease. During the 1890s the advantage of boiling milk as some protection against infection was beginning to be recognized. There was also a rapid increase in the sale of condensed milk which had the advantage that all germs were destroyed during its preparation.

Experiments had been made for some time in the production of condensed and dried milk. Condensed milk, to which sugar was added, was sold in tins in which the product was sterilized, and it proved to be a valuable way of using the skimmed milk which was left over in the butter factories. By about 1870 cheap tinned condensed milk was available in large quantities, and was bought by poor people especially to feed young children, and of course for use in tea instead of the dearer fresh milk. The condensed skimmed milk had almost no fat nor vitamins A and D in it, and was soon shown by doctors to be an unsatisfactory food for babies. In 1894, therefore, an Act of Parliament was passed making it compulsory for the tins to carry a label stating that condensed skimmed milk was unsuitable for feeding infants and young children. Experiments in dried and powdered milk were also made during the second half of the nineteenth century, and soon after 1900 modern-type milk powders came into use.

Tea

During the eighteenth and early nineteenth centuries, tea-drinking progressed from being the occasional luxury of prosperous town dwellers to becoming the national beverage of all classes. Tea consumption remained remarkably steady at an annual 1¼ to 1½ lbs (560-680 grams) per head of the population during the first half of the nineteenth century, in spite of the changes in prices. In Mincing Lane, London, wholesalers began to do their own blending, and the first proprietary blends of tea appeared with brand names which soon became household words. Most tea was still sold to the public loose from chests, and was often badly adulterated. Some grocers began to mix or blend teas from different chests to ensure their own standards of quality; many famous businesses started as tea blenders, among them Harrods, Fortnum & Mason, and Cadbury's. To combat fears of adulteration, John Horniman from the Isle of Wight had the idea in 1826 of selling tea in sealed quarter and half-pound packets, guaranteed to contain pure tea. The packets were made out of paper, and lined with lead. At first the tea was packed by hand, though later

Horniman invented a primitive packing machine. Other traders such as Mazawattee, Lipton's, Lyons and the Maypole Tea Company soon followed suit, and there was keen competition between the rival companies.

The adulteration of tea, however, remained big business until the Food and Drugs Act of 1875. Large quantities of 'tea' were manufactured from the leaves of ash, sloe and elder, gathered from English hedgerows and curled and coloured on copper plates. In the early years of the century, an official report estimated that 4 million pounds (1,800,000 kg) of this rubbish was faked and sold each year, as compared with only 6 million pounds of genuine tea imported by the East India Company. Some of the tea imported from China was already adulterated with used tea-leaves or other substances including dyes, chemicals and iron fillings. In 1851 *The Times* carried a report that Edward South and his wife of Camberwell, London, were 'busily engaged in the manufacture' of adulterated tea:

> There was an extensive furnace before which was suspended an iron pan containing sloe-leaves and tea-leaves which they were in the habit of purchasing from coffee-shop keepers after being used. On searching the place they found an immense quantity of used tea, bay-leaves and every description of spurious ingredients for the purpose of manufacturing illicit tea, and they were mixed with a solution of gums and a quantity of copperas ... they pursued their nefarious trade most extensively, and were in the habit of dealing largely with grocers, chandlers and others.

An investigation of 1872 found that 36 out of 41 samples of tea were grossly adulterated with such things as sand, magnetic iron, China clay, prussian blue and spurious leaves. Yet within the next few years adulteration of tea had all but disappeared. The Act of 1875 made the importing and sale of adulterated tea an offence, and allowed inspectors to seize and destroy such tea. As a result the situation improved rapidly.

The Tea Trade
Until the early years of the nineteenth century the East India Company had enjoyed a monopoly of the English tea trade with China. They had organized the cultivation of opium in India which they sold to the Chinese in return for tea and silk. Other merchants wanted a share in both the opium and tea trade, and in 1830 the government gave way to the vigorous criticism and abolished the monopoly. The East India Company looked for an alternative source of tea supplies, preferably one under their own control. They found it in Assam, in northern India. They no longer had a monopoly of trade in India but still controlled the administration of the country; the Charter Act of 1833 gave British subjects freedom to trade and settle in India. The cultivation of tea

51

began in Assam in 1834, and in 1839 the first eight chests of Indian tea were sold at the London auctions. The Assam Company, set up in 1840, had many years of difficulty; but, by the late 1850s, having given up the attempt to grow Chinese-type tea, it was successfully growing Indian tea.

The new tea from India was black tea. Early tea in Britain had been mostly high-quality Chinese green tea, but black tea from the Bohea Hills in China was also popular. Green tea is unfermented tea, drunk usually without milk or sugar, and is now very little drunk in England except in Chinese restaurants. Just as new sources of tea supply in India were being developed, there was much concern in England about the adulteration of tea, and public taste swung from green tea to black tea.

Even so, China remained a great tea producer; though her percentage share of the trade fell, her production of tea for export was still increasing, and only reached its peak in the 1880s. When the East India Company had begun its tea trade with China in the early eighteenth century, the Chinese Emperor allowed foreigners to trade only through the port of Canton, and only with a group of 13 Chinese merchants known as the 'hong merchants' because of their 'hongs' or warehouses near the 'factories' of the foreign merchants. There were 13 of these factories along the waterfront. Each flew its national flag, and each had its own dock from which sampans took chests of tea and bales of silk down river to the anchorage, ten miles (16 km) away, beyond which foreign ships were not allowed to pass.

In 1839 the Emperor of China gave instructions that the trade in 'foreign

32 A Chinese drawing of an 'Old Hairy One' or 'foreign devil', and English sailor in 1839, shortly before the outbreak of the Opium War between England and China.

mud' (opium) must be stopped. The trade was illegal but it was actively pursued by British merchants to enable them to obtain very profitable supplies of tea and silk, and by some Chinese merchants who also made great profits. Orders were issued to confiscate supplies of opium, and some 20,000 chests valued at more than £3 million were seized and burned. Chinese troops were sent to blockade the foreign factories. But the British refused to accept this, claiming that they were only supplying Chinese demands, and that it was the fault of the Chinese who refused to allow them to trade more freely. The Emperor appealed to the conscience of the British government in a letter to the 'young girl' at present ruling England (Queen Victoria). He recognized that foreigners 'could not live' without 'rhubarb, tea and silk', and was willing to allow these goods to be sold. 'But there is a class of foreigners that makes opium and brings it for sale, tempting fools to destroy themselves, merely in order to reap profit. Formerly the number of opium smokers was small, but now the vice has spread far and wide and the poison penetrated deeper and deeper.' He had therefore decided to inflict very severe penalties on opium dealers and smokers. It appeared, however, that the opium was manufactured 'by certain devilish persons in places subject to your [Queen Victoria's] rule. I am told that in your own country opium smoking is forbidden under severe penalties. This means you are aware how harmful it is.'

The British government was more concerned, however, about trading interests. In spite of criticism from politicians such as Mr Gladstone, who spoke of this 'infamous and atrocious business', the government was prepared

33 The British steamer *Medea* captures or destroys thirteen Chinese junks. The junks were slow-moving and cumbersome, and unfairly matched against the British 'fire devil'.

34 The *Ariel* and the *Taeping* neck-and-neck off the Lizard near the end of the Great Tea Race from China to London, 1866.

to go to war with the Chinese in order to enforce the opium trade. British warships were sent to Canton, and made several attacks on the South China coast, bombarding towns, looting and burning. The Chinese were soon defeated by the enemy's superior strength; by the Treaty of Nanking (1842), they were compelled to give Hong Kong to Britain and to open five Chinese ports to foreign trade. No mention was made of stopping the opium trade.

For the next 50 years the tea trade between China and Britain flourished. Some of the tea was sent overland by camel caravan, a journey of 11,000 miles (18,000 km) which took 16 months (when the Trans-Siberian railway was completed in 1904 it provided a simpler route). Most of the tea, however, was sent by sea, and a special type of merchant ship, much faster than the old East Indiaman, was developed to meet the need. This was the clipper, a three-masted, full-rigged vessel with a great turn of speed which was first developed in America. London tea merchants were amazed when in 1850 the American clipper, *Oriental*, reached England with a cargo of tea after a journey of only 97 days from Hong Kong. British clippers were soon built to compete with this. During the 1850s the Americans had cornered the market, but they lost ground during the American Civil War (1861-65).

A great annual race took place between the clippers who tried to be first home with the new season's crop. A prize of £500 was awarded to the captain and crew of the winning ship. Great profits were to be made as the new tea sold for as much as 3d a lb dearer than the tea from the slower ships. Great risks were taken by many captains, and many ships were lost. The most exciting race was in 1866 when three clippers, the *Ariel*, the *Taeping* and the *Serica* which set off on the same tide from Foochow all docked in London 99 days later on the same tide. This great race was, however, one of the last — the Suez Canal was opened in 1869 and large steamers became a more economic proposition. The final tea race was in 1871, after which most of the clippers were transferred to the Australian run, carrying emigrants outwards and wool homewards.

During the 1860s Indian tea plantations had expanded rapidly not only in Assam but in other parts of India; in the 1870s Ceylon became an important tea-producing area. The Indian tea was rather stronger than the China tea to which the British were accustomed, and to begin with it was often blended with China tea. In the early 1890s Britain still obtained about one-third of her tea from China, but merchants had to pay import duty on foreign tea, whereas the tea from India and Ceylon, part of the British Empire, was exempt from duty. By 1900 India had taken the place of China as the world's leading tea exporter, and Ceylon was not far behind in third place.

By the middle of the nineteenth century tea consumption was enormous and increasing; it rose from 1.6 lb (690 grams) per person per year in the decade 1841-50, to 5.7 lbs (2,600 grams) in 1891-1900. Tea and cakes in the afternoon for ladies at home became a British institution (the French called it *le five o'clock*). This in turn led to a demand for tea in cafés, hotels and even department stores. Some hotels had orchestras and provided the *thé dansant* (tea dance) where people could take tea and dance during the afternoon. But this was only for a small minority of prosperous, leisured people. For the rest companies such as the ABC (Aerated Bread Company) and J Lyons began to open tea rooms where respectable women and their children could have tea or a meal unescorted by their husbands, and where cheap meals were also provided for office workers. The first ABC opened in 1884 near London Bridge, and the first Lyons tea shop in Piccadilly in 1894. There were however, some anxieties about extensive tea-drinking. Beer had provided an important contribution to nutrition, whereas a large volume of hot fluid tended to reduce the intake of more nutritious foods. Poor people might in fact enjoy a deceptive feeling of warmth after drinking hot tea, when a glass of cold beer would have given them far more real food.

Coffee consumption also rose steadily; it doubled between 1850 and 1880 but then fell as tea became established as the national drink. In 1841 there were about 1,800 coffee shops in London for all classes including the poorest working men. A shop at St Giles for instance was selling coffee at 1½d a cup to about 1,500 men a day. The nineteenth-century coffee house was a much lower-class institution than the eighteenth-century one, whose upper-class customers now were members of the London Clubs. William Lovett, the Chartist leader, believed that the reduction in drunkenness he had witnessed during the first three decades of the nineteenth century was due mainly to the increase in the number of coffee houses and reading rooms. The consumption of cocoa was

35 Another non-alcoholic drink is given a high-powered recommendation!

also increasing rapidly, though it cost as much as 4d (1½p) a cup, and could only be found in the best class of coffee house. Cocoa was much advertised in teetotal papers, and was now manufactured by several Quaker temperance reformers — notably Cadbury's, Fry's and Rowntree's.

Soft Drinks

Alternatives to strong drink other than tea, coffee and cocoa could also be found during the nineteenth century. For instance a Dr Hooper of Hooper Struve developed non-intoxicating cordials. In the 1840s ginger beer and nettle beer were popular among working men in the north of England, and Henry Mayhew estimated that in London there were some 1,200 street sellers of ginger beer at 1d or ½d a glass. No intoxicating drinks were allowed to be sold at the Great Exhibition of 1851, so 1,092,337 bottles of Schweppes's soda water, lemonade and ginger beer were sold instead. Temperance speakers sometimes encouraged the sale of soft drinks at their meetings. Publicans began to stock cordials and drinks like ginger beer for teetotal customers, though it must be admitted that most customers wanted these drinks mixed with spirits.

7. Alcoholic Drinks, 1800~1900

Large-Scale Brewing

During the eighteenth century the government first encouraged the manufacture and sale of cheap gin, and then, faced with an outcry about its effects on health, restricted sales and taxed it heavily. There may, however, have been an ulterior motive for the taxation of gin, for it proved a most valuable source of government revenue. By the end of the eighteenth century spirit-drinking, though still a problem, was under control. Ale and beer were the chief national drinks, whether 'old', 'brown', 'pale' or 'three-thread', a mixture of all three. In the 1720s a new dark, strongly-hopped beer was developed which had the quality of 'three-thread' but came from a single barrel. It was a great favourite with market porters and became known as porter. London brewers specialized in porter. Dublin was famous for stout, while Burton- on-Trent, where the hard water was particularly suitable for brewing beer, was noted for a dry draught ale, strongly flavoured with hops and known as bitter.

Until the eighteenth century brewing was mainly done by individual inns or in the home, but by 1750 many breweries still famous today, such as Whitbread's, Guinness's and Barclay's, had been founded. William Cobbett, a supporter of country pursuits, lamented the evidence given by a Sussex farmer in 1821, 'that forty years ago there was not a labourer in this parish that did not brew his own beer; and that now there is not one that does it'. The breweries were up-to-date in their methods — they were for instance among the first customers for James Watt's steam engines — and their beer was of a standard quality. In 1815 eleven leading breweries were producing 2 million gallons (9 million litres) a year, a fifth of the national production; these leading brewers met together regularly to fix the price and strength of porter.

Consumption of Beer

It is difficult to estimate at all accurately how much beer was drunk in England in the early years of the nineteenth century because official figures only cover public and not private brewing. However, it seems (from figures worked out on malt consumption) that there was a steady fall in consumption from 33.9 gallons (150 litres) per head each year at the beginning of the century to 19.9 gallons (89 litres) in 1851; but then consumption increased again to 28 gallons (127 litres) in 1865 and 34.4 gallons (156 litres), the highest point in the century, in 1876. This amounted to an expenditure in 1825 of nearly £3 a year for every man, woman and child in the country, or £15 for every household. As wages were low (often much less than £1 a week), even the average expenditure

36 (*Above*) An engraving of an eighteenth-century London brewery.

38 (*Opposite*) The impressive scale of the Guinness brewery in Dublin in the nineteenth century.

37 (*Below*) Large-scale brewing at Barclay and Perkins Brewery. Barrels were loaded on to drays that were dragged by handsome, well-groomed cart-horses for delivery to publicans.

JAMES'S GATE PORTER BREWERY
DUBLIN

GUINNESS'S
DOUBLE
STOUT

on drink was enough to keep many families poor.

There are many reasons why alcoholic drinks were so widely drunk in the first half of the nineteenth century. First of all beer was drunk as a thirst-quencher, safer than the polluted water that was all that was available for most people (see pages 38-45). Milk too was a dangerous drink (pages 46-50). Tea, coffee and cocoa were more expensive than alcoholic drinks although they gradually came down in price. For instance, in 1840, Londoners could buy coffee for 1½d a cup, tea for 2d, but porter for only 2½d a pint. Alcoholic drinks were believed to help physical stamina, and it was thought impossible to work for instance as a blacksmith or get in the harvest without plenty of beer. Alcohol was also a pain-killer, dulling the edge of physical pain and mental strain.

Another major factor was the social life provided by the public house — the light, warmth, recreation and company not available in the ordinary home. It was a local meeting-place for political clubs, trade unions and friendly societies, and was a centre where news could be exchanged and trading deals agreed. There were four kinds of establishments selling drinks. In descending order of respectability they were — the 'inn', which also provided accommodation and food for the traveller; the 'tavern' catering for the casual drinker; the 'ale-house' which supplied beer, but no spirits; and the 'gin shop'. Until 1830, all four had to have a licence from a magistrate. In 1830, however, the Sale of Beer Act made it legal for anyone to sell beer retail if they paid an excise fee of 2 guineas (£2.10).

'The new Beer Bill has begun its operations. Everyone is drunk,' wrote the Reverend Sydney Smith, Canon of St Paul's, in October 1830. 'Those who are not singing are sprawling. The sovereign people are in a beastly state.' This was probably an exaggeration, but there is no doubt that the effect of the Act was dramatic. Queues of those anxious to pay the 2-guinea fee formed up outside the excise offices. In Liverpool, 50 new beer-houses were opened every day for several weeks. By the end of the year, there were 24,000 beer-houses in England and Wales, and by 1836 the number had nearly doubled. There was also an increase in the number of licensed premises.

The government's intention in passing the Sale of Beer Act was to provide an alternative to the gin shop, and give 'the poor and working classes of the community a chance of obtaining a better, cheaper and more wholesome beverage.' As well as doing away with licensing, they proposed also to abolish the duty on beer. Free trade in beer, they hoped, would result in competition that would raise the quality of beer. Much beer had been adulterated and watered down, and the people would now have, said the Lord Chancellor, 'good beer instead of bad spirits'. Indeed it might be said that the government was giving them 'a moral species of beverage'. The Prime Minister himself, the Duke of Wellington, moved the Bill's Second Reading, claiming that there was no real danger of 'disturbance and riot' when the price of a quart pot of beer fell from 5d to 3d.

But the Duke of Wellington's Beer Bill, as it was commonly known, did not do much to prevent adulteration. A price war broke out between the established inns and taverns and the new beer-shops. The inns which also sold spirits cut their prices to an unprofitable level in an attempt to drive the beer-shops out of existence, and the beer-shops replied by watering down and adulterating their beer. Adulteration had been common before the Act, but now there was a general substitution of drugs instead of malt and hops, and many substances, some of them poisonous, were added to watered beer to give the illusion of strength. The chemist Frederick Accum's 'Treatise' on the Adulteration of Food and Culinary Poisons' revealed that whereas the average alcoholic strength of London porter bought from the breweries was 5.25 per cent, it averaged only 4.5 per cent when bought from the public house. Many public houses were 'tied' to particular breweries and it is claimed that they gave such unfavourable terms to their tenants that they were forced to adulterate the brew in order to make a living. As a result of much public disquiet a select Parliamentary Commission on food adulteration was set up in 1855 which led to the passing of the first Food and Drugs Act in 1860.

When the Beer Act was passed in 1830 there was little objection from religious or other bodies to beer-drinking as such. In fact beer was seen as a temperance drink and any attacks on drunkenness were made against spirit-drinking. However, after 1830 beer-shops came under attack from clergymen and magistrates, who were often more concerned about the gambling, cruel sports and political activity which went on in beer-shops, rather than the effects of beer-drinking. The consumption per head of beer did rise to a modest extent after the Act between 1834 and 1839, and then resumed its downward trend.

Although the beer-house continued to come under fire it took nearly 40 years to bring about a change in the law. By then, beer-houses numbered 53,000, and were spreading at the rate of 2,000 a year. In 1869 the Wine and Beer-House Act made it necessary to obtain a magistrate's licence to open a new beer-house, and in 1880 the beer duty was reintroduced. Thus ended the free trade in beer, and incidentally the Beer Act of 1830 which the Duke of Wellington had considered a greater achievement than any of his military victories.

Gin-Palaces

The consumption of beer may have gone down in the nineteenth century, but the consumption of spirits went up; there was a slight drop immediately after 1830 but by 1838 spirit sales were higher and by 1845 very much higher. To compete with the beer-houses 'gin-palaces' were introduced, and provided attractive surroundings in which to sell the more expensive product. The gin-palace brought some colour and glitter into social life, making gin a more respectable drink for the middle-classes. In *Sketches by Boz* (published in 1836) Dickens describes a typical gin-palace:

The gay building with a fantastically ornamental parapet, the illuminated clock, the plate-glass windows surrounded by stucco rosettes and its profusion of gas lights in richly gilt burners, is perfectly dazzling when contrasted with the darkness and dirt we have just left. A bar of french-polished mahogany, elegantly carved, extends the whole width of the place; there are two aisles of great casks, painted green and gold, enclosed with a light brass rail and bearing such descriptions as 'Old Tom', 'Young Tom', 'Samson' . . . Beyond the bar is a lofty and spacious saloon, full of the same enticing vessels with a gallery running round it, equally well-furnished.

The gin-palaces were immensely popular with the public but were viewed with great misgiving by many social reformers and by the increasingly powerful temperance movement.

The Golden Age of Wine, and Disaster Overcome

The nineteenth century has been called the 'Golden Age' of wine. The great estates in the wine-producing countries were making fine wine regardless of the cost. It was bought by the wealthy and discerning who had time and space to lay it down to mature for 20 or 30 years. There were a series of superb vintages, especially of clarets, and wine-tasting became a business for connoisseurs.

But then the blow fell. European vineyards were devastated by the American vine-louse, a sort of aphis, which attacked the roots of the vines and caused the plants to wither and die. The phylloxera beetle first appeared in France in the 1860s, probably imported on an American vine, and soon the plague had spread throughout the country, causing the most appalling damage. Within 20 years nearly all the vines in France had been killed, and it looked like the end of European wine. Then it was discovered that the roots of American vines were immune to phylloxera; people realized that it would be possible to import millions of American vine-stocks and graft on to them the remaining cuttings of the European vines. The idea worked, and the European vineyards flourished again.

The Victorians took their wine drinking seriously and raised it to a fine art. It was an age of great vintage wines carefully laid down and meticulously served. Clubs for 'gentlemen' grew in number, their cellars stocked with fine wines. The emphasis was on quality, rather than the previous century's somewhat brutish accent on quantity. Drinking spirits, apart from brandy, was

39 The nineteenth-century gin-palace was higher up the social scale than the eighteenth-century gin shops, though the campaign against strong drink was mounting.

40 A dinner of the Dilettante Society, a club of prosperous men who cultivated a taste for fine vintage wines.

considered low class. There was no place for wives in these drinking rites. Men stayed late at their clubs, and did not take their wives out to restaurants. Even when they dined in private houses, the ladies would retire after the meal while the men stayed in the dining room circulating port and brandy until a late hour.

Mr Gladstone helped to encourage the fashion for fine wines when he negotiated the Cobden-Gladstone Treaty with France in 1860. This reduced the duty payable on French wines, and cut the price of a bottle of wine by about a third. Gladstone also licensed grocers to sell wine which could be bought for as little as 1sh 6d (7½p) a bottle. Although this was mocked at by the upper classes as being grocer's claret and port, it proved extremely popular, and meant that for the first time wine was no longer an exclusively upper-class drink. At the turn of the century a more frivolous note was introduced by the preference shown by the Prince of Wales (soon to be Edward VII) for lighter drinks such as Chablis, hock and seltzer, and dry champagne. High society followed his example. Poorer people drank beer, which was stronger than today's brews. By now the favourite drink was mild and bitter, or powerful stout diluted with beer to make porter at 3d (1p) a quart.

8. The Temperance Movement

Criticism of over-indulgency in strong drink had been voiced since earliest times, and some religious leaders, like Mohammed, had been such strong opponents that alcohol was expressly forbidden to their followers. But it was not until the early years of the nineteenth century that there was any organized temperance movement in Britain. By then the worst excesses of the gin epidemic had been controlled, but social reformers began to condemn the evils of spirit-drinking, and temperance societies sprang up. These societies did not at this stage try to prevent the drinking of beer — indeed beer was considered almost as a temperance drink, and a much safer drink than the impure water supplies that were all that was otherwise available. The emphasis of the temperance movement was on moderation, and the avoidance of 'hard' drinks, meaning spirits.

The Anti-Spirits Movement

The temperance movement began in the United States in the 1770s and spread to Europe about 30 years later. Ireland was the first country to follow the American lead; it was a poor country but its annual expenditure on spirits of about £6 million was much more than it could afford. Members of a Temperance Society in Wexford signed a pledge that 'the use of intoxicating spirits . . . forms intemperate habits and appetites'. The members 'do agree to refrain from the use of distilled spirits, except as medicine in the case of bodily ailment; that we will not allow the use of them in our families, nor provide them for the entertainment of our friends, and that we will, in all suitable ways, discountenance the use of them in the community at large.' The pledge, which prohibited the use of spirits as opposed to beer, and even allowed spirits if they were considered a medical necessity, was typical of the views of early temperance societies. In Belfast, Dr John Edgar, the founder of the Ulster Temperance Society, launched the organization in 1829 by pouring all the whisky in his house, almost a gallon (4.5 litres), out of his parlour window into the courtyard below.

In England the temperance movement was often connected with the Friendly Societies to which workers contributed to give themselves some sort of insurance against sickness and unemployment. To begin with these societies usually met in public houses, but this led to members spending their money on drink instead of on their subscriptions, so some societies made temperance a condition of membership, and met in private homes or in meeting houses they built for themselves. In the 1820s the social climate was favourable for the

temperance movement. The Industrial Revolution was beginning to raise the standard of living for the working classes, and a responsible body of men, ready to campaign for the right to vote and to form trade unions, grew up in the towns. These men often spent their very limited leisure-time furthering their education at the Mechanics' Institutes, and were frequently active Non-conformists. Naturally they deplored the degrading effect of drunkenness on working people.

The new cheapness and availability of tea and coffee, and the fact that these used boiled water, made an important contribution to the trend away from strong drink. Water was actually worsening in quality at the time the temperance movement was being founded, but the early reformers encouraged the drinking of tea and coffee at their social gatherings. The 1820s also saw the first active interest of women in the temperance movement — it was they and their children who suffered if the father of the family became a drunkard, so they were naturally keen supporters of any society which might discourage drinking.

Drunkenness was becoming unfashionable. 'No person who has lived so long as I have,' William Huskisson (1770-1830) declared in the House of Commons, 'but must perceive that a greater degree of sobriety prevails amongst the lower classes than was formerly the case.' A major contribution to this trend was made by the great temperance pioneers, notably Dr John Edgar, John Dunlop and William Collins. In 1829, Edgar founded the Ulster Temperance Society, Dunlop started a moderation society in Greenock, and Collins launched the Scottish Temperance Society. By the end of 1830 temperance had clearly taken root in Scotland; half-a-million pamphlets had been distributed, 130 societies formed, and 25,000 members enrolled. Temperance societies were set up in Bradford, Manchester, Leeds, Bolton, Birmingham, Newcastle and Bristol. The London Temperance Society was created in November 1830, and the following year it became the British and Foreign Temperance Society with the Bishop of London as its president. Often campaigns against drink were only one aspect of a general movement to improve conditions for the poor; some

41 (*Opposite*) A temperance broadsheet of the 1830s claiming that shipwrecks are often caused by drunkeness, that most of the inmates of prisons are drunkards, and that working-class violence stems from the consumption of spirits.

42 (*Left*) A sombre picture of the 'Drunkard's home', with its poverty and his frightened wife and child, drawn by George Cruikshank, an ardent supporter of the temperance cause.

temperance leaders also campaigned for free libraries, schools, public parks and open spaces, and for Friendly Societies which would provide sickness benefits, burial grants and medical care. On the whole, the temperance movement was supported mainly by the middle-class; working men, who were the chief victims of drink, were barely affected.

Total Abstinence — 'Drink Water'

Until about 1830, the temperance movement concerned itself solely with a campaign against spirit-drinking. The next stage, however, was dissatisfaction with moderation, and the preaching of total abstinence, that is the giving up of all intoxicating drink. In 1832 Joseph Livesey of Preston spelled it out clearly:

A man who drinks a quart of ale will take nearly two ounces of pure spirit . . . nearly equal to half a gill of brandy . . . It may be asked, if you deprive people of spirits, wine, ale, porter, cider, perry etc, what must they drink? . . . Drink . . . we would say, water if you would be wise, virtuous, happy and healthy; or if you will gratify your palate, a little coffee, tea, lemonade or any other undistilled and unfermented liquor.

This new stand had arisen when Livesey and his friend John King challenged each other to give up 'drink' altogether. They then persuaded five others of the Preston Temperance Society to sign a pledge which read: 'We agree to abstain from all liquors of an Intoxicating Quality, whether Ale, Porter, Wine or Ardent Spirits, except as medicine.' These 'Seven Men of Preston' became the heroes of the total abstinence movement which preached with religious fervour: 'Malt not, brew not, distil not, buy not, sell not, drink not.' It was about this time that the word 'teetotal' was coined, to contrast with what Livesey called this 'moderation botheration pledge'.

Further temperance societies now sprang up, the most famous being the Independent Order of Rechabites and the Phoenix Societies. Between them they attracted numerous members. It was almost a mark of respectability to

67

belong to a temperance society — Queen Victoria became Patron of the British and Foreign Temperance Society in the first year of her reign. Moreover, the societies provided the opportunity for social life without the need to visit public houses or gin-palaces. The Phoenix Society, for instance, ran coffee shops which stayed open late at night and where men could play cards and dominoes.

Probably the greatest temperance reformer of all time was a Catholic priest, Father Mathew, who started his crusade against drink in Ireland in 1838. Although an ordinary-looking man with a weak and shrill voice, he was a great orator whose sermons had a startling effect on drinking habits in Ireland. One of his gimmicks was to ask a series of questions, getting the audience to shout the replies: 'What does a racehorse drink? Water! What does the elephant drink? Water! What does the lion drink? Water!' His meetings were packed — bars emptied and slum streets became peaceful — and people queued up to sign the temperance pledge. In three months it was claimed that 25,000 had signed, in five months 131,000, and by the end of the year nearly 200,000, though it is now believed that these figures were exaggerated by enthusiastic supporters. The consumption of spirits in Ireland fell in four years from 12,300,000 gallons in 1838 to 7,400,000 gallons in 1840 and to only 5,300,000 in 1842. It was claimed that there were then 5 million on the teetotal roll out of a population of 8 million, which again seems like an exaggeration. Breweries and distilleries went out of business during this time of temperance mania; drunkenness virtually disappeared, and the serious-crime rate dropped sharply. A secretary of a mining company in County Waterford where a thousand employees had signed the pledge reported:

43 Father Mathew making his temperance pledge to the well-known Irish politician, Daniel O'Connell, MP.

From being a most dissolute, idle and intractable set of workers . . . clothed in rags and living in many respects worse . . . even than the beasts of the field, they are now the most industrious, orderly and well-clad people in the Empire.

Father Mathew continued his mission in Scotland and England with similar success. It was reported that during one ten-week visit, he made 600,000 teetotallers; he was also a great hit with London society including Sir Robert Peel and the Duke of Wellington. On his death in 1856, a statue was erected to him in Dublin which shows him looking towards the bridge and with his back turned on the numerous grog shops which were now flourishing again.

An attempt was made in the 1840s to enlist the support of young people for the temperance cause. The Band of Hope was founded by Jabez Tunnicliff in 1847 for children under 16. They had to make the simple pledge: 'I do agree that I will not use intoxicating liquors as a beverage' (though some societies also mentioned tobacco, snuff and opium to be on the safe side). By 1874 there were at least 5,500 Bands of Hope with 800,000 members; by 1889, 16,000 societies and two million members, and by 1897, 3,200,000 members. One reason for the Band of Hope's popularity was the variety of interesting activities — singing, sightseeing trips, magic-lantern talks, games etc — that it offered at a time when there was little organized entertainment for children. Although many children lapsed from their pledge when they became adults, there is no doubt that the society contributed to a considerable increase in anti-drink attitudes during the last quarter of the nineteenth century.

Thomas Cook (who later founded the famous travel agency) was a

44 Eloquent expressions on the faces of two visitors to the Great Exhibition of 1851 on finding that no alcoholic drinks could be bought in the refreshment rooms.

temperance supporter who undertook to organize the travel arrangements for members who wished to attend a great temperance demonstration in the midlands. Next he brought teetotallers up from the country on a cheap excursion to march in procession to the Great Exhibition of 1851, and later attend a great fête at London Zoo. It was incidentally a triumph for the movement that alcohol was banned from the refreshment rooms of the 'Crystal Palace'.

Division and Discord

Considerable differences of opinion on both principles and policy, together with great intolerance among members, inevitably slowed down the growth in membership of the temperance movement. Different religious persuasions competed with each other, and there were even atheists and freethinkers who argued that references in the Bible condoning strong drink proved how bad a guide to conduct the Bible was. However, on the whole, religion and temperance went hand in hand, and the movement tended to preach to the converted rather than do missionary work.

In the 1850s the movement divided into two parts — the 'moral persuasionists' who aimed at defeating drink by persuading everyone to sign the pledge; and the 'prohibitionists' who favoured making the manufacture and sale of drink illegal. The latter group were particularly influenced by the introduction at this time of prohibition into the State of Maine in the USA. The United Kingdom Alliance (for the Suppression of the Traffic in all Intoxicating Liquors) was formed in 1853, and took the prohibitionist line. They claimed that they did not want to stop men drinking — they would make no attempt to stop a man from brewing his own beer or importing his own wine — but that they wanted to get rid of the 'accursed trade', the 'cursed traffic', in strong drink. The Alliance held demonstrations presided by dramatic and emotional speakers. John B Gough was one of the star turns. Holding up a glass of water he would declaim:

> Here is our beautiful beverage, water, pure water . . . There is no necessity to drink, except to quench one's thirst . . . Did you never lift the goblet of pure water to your lips and feel it trickling over the tongue and gurgling down the throat? . . . Our beverage is beautiful and pure, for God brewed it, not in the distillery but out of the earth . . . Beautiful water! See how it wears a golden gauze for the setting sun and silvery tissue for the midnight moon! . . . It never broke a mother's heart . . . Never did pale-faced wife or starving child . . . weep into it a bitter tear; never did drunkard howl back from his death-bed a fearful curse upon it.

But the National Temperance League tried to discredit Gough in a court case which claimed that he took drink and drugs; as a result the whole movement became seriously divided.

Sunday Closing

All sections of the temperance movement, however, agreed to oppose the opening of public houses on Sundays. 'Sunday drinking', said the Bishop of Lincoln in 1870, 'meant misery in this world and eternal shame and sorrow in the world to come . . . Publicans . . . knew their souls were in peril so long as they continued to sell liquors on the Lord's day.'

Since 1828 the law had required public houses to close during the hours of divine service, but this regulation was widely ignored. At other times it had an effect that was not intended: 'Last Sunday I had occasion to walk through Broadway at a few minutes before eleven o'clock,' reported Mr George Wilson, giving evidence in 1834 before a House of Commons Select Committee. 'I found the pavement before every gin-shop crowded; just as church time approached, the gin-shops sent forth their multitudes, swearing and fighting and bawling obscenely; some were stretched on the pavement insensibly drunk while every few steps the footway was taken up by drunken wretches being dragged to the station-house by the police.' In 1839 an act was passed closing

45 George Cruikshank's version of the 'Battle of A-gin-court'. Though a keen teetotaller, Cruikshank kept a sense of humour on the subject.

all drink shops from midnight on Saturday until 1 pm on Sunday. It was extremely effective as can be shown by the fact that convictions for drunkenness in London fell from 21,237 to 8,321 over the next five years.

There was now great pressure from the temperance movement for complete Sunday closing as existed in Scotland, but there was also strong resistance from the drink trade and its customers. In 1854 the Sale of Beer Act greatly restricted hours of Sunday opening. However, as a result of riots and demonstrations, a further Act increasing Sunday licensing hours to 1 pm-3 pm and 5 pm-11 pm was passed a year later. This was a major defeat for the teetotallers who continued to campaign for Sunday closing without success in England, though they did achieve complete Sunday closing in Wales and Scotland.

One of the positive measures in the temperance campaign was the provision of alternatives to the public house. For instance the Metropolitan Free Drinking Fountain Association set up in 1859 provided hundreds of public drinking fountains. Other reformers tried to compete with the public house by providing the Coffee Public House 'where good coffee and tea . . . take the place of beer and gin'. Temperance hotels were another development.

Prohibition?

Sir Wilfred Lawson, a staunch supporter of the temperance cause, was elected to the House of Commons in 1859. He attacked the licensed trade and the House of Lords which he declared was 'full of thick-headed fellows . . . who had brewed a lot of beer.' He anticipated strong opposition from the Upper House, whom he referred to as 'the beerage', to his Bill to enable householders to prohibit the sale of intoxicating drinks in their district if a two-thirds majority wished it. His Bill, however, was soundly defeated. But there were strong feelings in the country about whether or not there should be prohibition. In 1872, when the government's Permissive Licensing Bill was being debated, Dr William Magee, later Archbishop of York, declared: 'If I must take my choice . . . I should say it would be better that England should be free, than that England should be compulsorily sober.' Yet Dr Magee went on to preside over the annual meeting of the Church of England Temperance Reformation Society, where he spoke of drunkenness as 'the canker eating into the very heart of our nation'. Dr Magee thought that the cause for local option was inconsistent. Either the liquor trade was right or it was wrong, and if wrong then it should be forbidden everywhere. He declared it would be far better to campaign for sanitary reform, since the teetotallers told 'men to drink water but . . . in many places for water they were given diluted sewage'.

An argument against prohibition which infuriated teetotallers was that it would wreck the national economy by cutting off overnight the £30 million a year licence fees, and the vast liquor taxation which amounted to almost a third of the national budget. The Inland Revenue seemed to think, complained

46 (*Left*) The National Temperance Festival held at Crystal Palace in 1872.

47 (*Right*) A demonstration against the Liberal Licensing Bill marching along the Embankment, London, in 1908.

Sir Wilfred Lawson, that 'the great object for which a man was sent into the world was to consume duty-paid liquor'. The lost money, the prohibitionists declared, could easily be made up by savings on workhouses and prisons, and by abandoning foreign wars.

But prohibition, even as a matter of local choice, was too strong a measure for most of the population, and instead a number of restrictions and controls were introduced. An Act in 1869 reversed the policy of the 1830 Beer Act by making all the retail trade in beer and wine subject to supervision by the licensing authorities. Further acts laid down rules forbidding gambling and drunkenness in public houses, and the sale of drink to children. By this time the issue of drink had become something of a political question, causing splits within the parties as well as between them. There was, however, more support for the brewers and distillers in the Conservative Party, while a substantial section of the Liberal Party and Trade Union MPs were non-drinkers. 'We have been borne down in a torrent of gin and beer', said Gladstone when the Liberals were defeated at the polls.

The temperance movement next tried to achieve a reduction in the number of public houses. The story was constantly told on their platforms of the working man who had to pass 20 public houses on his way home from work; on pay day he could pass 19 but the twentieth was one too many, so he came home drunk and with empty pockets week after week. They argued therefore that a reduction in the number of licences would reduce the amount of drunkenness! In 1908 the House of Lords refused to pass the Liberal Licensing Bill which the Conservatives claimed would ruin the brewery trade and to which public opinion vigorously objected. Five months later Lloyd George introduced his famous Budget which the Lords also rejected, but this time they had taken a step in the direction of self-destruction.

9. Two Wars and the Years Between

The outbreak of war on 4 August 1914 presented the temperance movement with both a challenge and an opportunity. At first there was an understandable tendency to stand drinks for the brave boys in uniform, or to keep up one's spirits in the public house. Pubs in London were open from five in the morning until half past midnight, and in other English towns from 6 am to 10 pm; there was soon a feeling that in wartime this was intolerable. It was clearly undesirable to have army and navy recruits coming on duty in a state of drunkenness, and soon the threat drink posed to war production became very evident.

The first step taken by the government was to restrict the opening hours of public houses in military and naval districts, a step which was criticized as 'waving the flag and seeking to advance by a side wind the cause of temperance'. By the end of 1914 restricted hours were in operation in half the licensing districts in England and Wales, and the reduction in drunkenness was remarkable. Even the *Brewers' Gazette* admitted that there had been 'a transformation of the night scenes of London so that many once rowdy areas have suddenly become peaceful and respectable'. Early in 1915 a London jury was told that 'the closing of the public houses at 10 o'clock has undoubtedly produced a wonderful result'.

Over the four-year period of the war, two major Acts of Parliament caused a revolution in Britain's drinking habits. Control of licensing hours now extended to 38 million people out of a total of 41 million, and it was only in a few remote country districts that it was still possible to drink from dawn to dusk.

The temperance movement naturally welcomed the licensing restrictions, but they were much less in favour of another government measure, whereby drink was more heavily taxed. This they had always disliked because they believed that the government would become dependent on the revenue from drink, and unwilling to introduce temperance reforms. In November 1914, Lloyd George increased duty on beer by a halfpenny on the half-pint. It could now be seen as a patriotic gesture to drink beer — 'Drink the national beverage and help your country!' read a brewer's advertisement. 'Order a pint of beer and drive a nail into the Kaiser's coffin. If you can't manage a pint order half a pint and drive in a tin-tack!' But Lloyd George also had the idea of making beer weaker, and pursued a policy of high taxation on alcoholic drinks, the dilution of spirits, and the encouragement of lighter beers. By 1920 taxation had put spirits into the luxury class at four or five times the pre-war price. Beer, drastically reduced in strength and known mockingly as 'government ale', rose to 7d (3p) a pint, of which half went in taxation.

48 'Drinks for our brave boys' presented a problem during the Boer War and the First World War.

Although it was recognized that their motives were no doubt patriotic, the public were begged not to treat men in the armed forces to a drink. A young VC at Lincoln, it was reported, found 120 pints of beer, paid for by his neighbours, waiting for him at his local when he came home on leave; while three convalescent soldiers at Sheffield who had been lavishly treated were found lying incapable on the tramlines. 'Treating' was made illegal which, as the Bootle Chief Constable put it, got rid of the 'public-house bummer'. Teetotallers were very disturbed by the number of young men who broke the pledge on enlisting, and they conducted a vigorous campaign against the rum ration being issued to the troops. Temperance journals had advertisements of soldiers in shell holes drinking Fry's cocoa, though one MP alleged that this campaign was run and paid for by the cocoa firms.

However, far more serious than drinking at the Front was drinking at home, especially among shipyard and munition workers who earned high wages. Absenteeism and inefficiency were blamed on hangovers. In one shell factory alone, it was estimated in 1915 that a tenth of the normal working hours was lost through drink, while in the shipyards where working hours were very long, a loss of a third of the normal output was said to be common. 'Drink is doing more damage in the war than all the German submarines put together', declared the Prime Minister. 'We are fighting Germany, Austria and drink, and the greatest of these deadly foes is drink.'

One idea explored by Lloyd George was to nationalize the drink trade. It was estimated that it would cost £250 million to buy out every brewery and public house in England and Wales, which could then be run jointly as a public service. The Cabinet, however, felt unable to support such a controversial measure as state ownership, and instead created a Central Liquor Control Board with wide powers to limit opening hours, ban spirits, and introduce any other regulations necessary. Licensing hours now became shorter than at any time in British history, spirits were diluted, and in a few instances 'state pubs' were opened.

The 'Carlisle experiment' was the most famous example of state-run public houses. A vast munitions industry had been established in the town and, during the first half of 1916, there were eight times as many convictions for drunkenness and assaults on the police as the year before. The Central Liquor Control Board took over all but 47 of the 368 licensed premises. Three out of five breweries were closed, 123 public houses stopped selling alcoholic drink, and the remaining publicans became salaried managers paid by the state. The idea was to serve food and raise the whole status of the public house as a social centre. Billiard tables, bowling greens, newspapers, pianos, gramophones and film shows were provided. By March 1918 the Carlisle Scheme was making more profit than most private companies, and drunkenness in the town had been greatly reduced. (The Carlisle State Management Scheme remained in operation until very recent times when its 150 public houses and its brewery were sold off to private buyers.)

Before the end of the First World War the prohibitionists made one further attack on the liquor trade. A shortage of food led to their new slogan: 'Bread before beer'. It was 'little short of treason to the state', they claimed, to waste cereals in making drink. Beer production had in fact been reduced from a pre-war 36 million barrels to 26 million by 1916, and when in 1917 the government proposed a further reduction to 10 million barrels there was considerable popular unrest. The government decided, therefore, to approve the brewing of a further 6 million gallons (27 million litres) of light beer.

In fact the case for further restrictions and control of the liquor trade had evaporated. The nation had become more temperate. Consumption of alcohol had dropped from 89 million gallons (400 million litres) in 1914 to 37 million gallons (168 million litres) in 1918; cases of drunkenness in England and Wales had fallen from 184,000 to 29,000, and deaths from alcoholism had been cut by five-sixths. A manager of a men's lodging house in Newcastle said he now led 'a gentlemen's life' as he only had to collect four dozen (48) empty bottles on his daily rounds instead of his previous three gross (432). Children did not gather outside the public houses on Saturday nights to see the drunks thrown out, and anxious women did not have to search the gutters for their drunken husbands. 'The great masses of the people do not wish to go back to the old state of things . . . to the sort of squalor which used to be found three or four years ago', said a Member of Parliament.

After the war there was a period when the country felt in the mood for celebration, especially the 'gay young things' who were lucky enough to have survived the war. For some of the wealthy it was a hectic round of cocktail parties and night clubs, of jazz, the Charleston and fast cars. The older generation was deeply concerned about what the younger generation was coming to. Noel Coward summed it up in his *Words and Music*:

> The gin is lasting out
> No matter whose
> We're merely casting out
> The Blues
> For Gin, in cruel
> Sober Truth
> Supplies the fuel
> For Flaming Youth.

To beat the licensing laws night clubs were opened where members could buy their own drinks at very high prices and drink there all night on the grounds that these were private parties.

49 A 1920s party.

Prohibition

Just as the authorities in Britain were beginning to discuss the possible end of wartime drinking restrictions, prohibition of all alcoholic drink was introduced into the United States of America in the Eighteenth Amendment to the Constitution, January 1920. Teetotallers in Britain hoped we might follow suit, but the mobbing of visiting American speakers soon made it clear that public opinion here was strongly opposed. The Licensing Act of 1921 made many of the wartime restrictions permanent, including limited hours of opening and an afternoon closure; beer and spirits never regained their pre-war strength, and high prices had come to stay.

Meanwhile in America the Prohibition Commissioner declared:

This law will be obeyed in cities, large and small, and in villages, and where it is not obeyed it will be enforced. The law says that liquor to be used as a beverage must not be manufactured. We shall see that it is not manufactured. Not sold nor given away, nor hauled in anything on the surface of the earth nor in the air.

This well-meant Puritan reform, however, was to transform American social life in a very different way from what had been intended. Instead of making the country more sober and law-abiding, the ban encouraged gangsterism and crime, since vast fortunes could be made out of the sale of illegal drink. The most law-abiding American citizens now became obsessed with getting hold of liquor and visiting 'speak-easies'; as Groucho Marx quipped: 'I was TT [teetotal] until Prohibition.' In one year of Prohibition the citizens of the United States consumed 200 million gallons (900 million litres) of malt liquor and 118 million gallons (540 million litres) of wine, while the professional bootleggers earned themselves an income of 4,000 million dollars.

Liquor was smuggled into the country by land and sea. Much of it was made illegally and some of it was extremely dangerous, even deadly. Gangsters like Al Capone in Chicago made a mockery of law and order, and gang warfare sprang up between rival gangs. There were over 700 gangland assassinations during the period of Prohibition. By 1930 over half-a-million Americans had been arrested for drink offences (though they were mostly small-time offenders caught drinking, not the big-time operators), and between them were sentenced to a total of 33,000 years in prison. In the same period 35,000 people died from drinking poisonous liquor and many more were permanently incapacitated. In Chicago alone convictions for drunken driving rose by 475 per cent, and deaths from alcoholism by 600 per cent. By 1933 America had had enough; the Democratic Party swept into power with a slogan of 'A New Deal and a pot of beer for everyone'.

The events taking place in America put a stop to any serious call for

50 The announcement of Prohibition: bottles of wines and spirits are hurled against this wall in Boston, USA, in 1920.

51 Gangster Al Capone and two of his henchmen. Capone made a fortune out of the ill-advised attempt of the US government to prohibit the sale of alcohol. The government found it difficult to convict him of any of his crimes except tax evasion.

52 The calming effect of a nice cup of tea brought round by a Salvation Army lady after a bomb has damaged the family home, 1940.

prohibition in Britain. Membership of the temperance societies fell sharply. The economic depression of the 1930s struck a further blow at the temperance movement — the millions of hungry unemployed were not very impressed by the evils of drink which they could not afford to buy.

During the Second World War (1939-45) there was no need to take measures to prevent damage to war production because of drink, as had been necessary during the First World War; nor was there need to discourage 'treating' members of the armed forces in pubs. By this time the heavy drinking of the past had largely disappeared, and any possible problem solved itself since strong drink was in very short supply. Spirits were severely rationed and could often only be obtained 'under the counter' (for favoured customers) or on the black market. In the ten years following 1939, the amount of whisky consumed on the home market fell by over 25 million bottles, and consumption of gin and other spirits fell as dramatically. There was no opportunity to import Continental wines so stocks fell rapidly. Even the beer got weaker.

Tea and Coffee
During each of the two World Wars, tea was the standby of the British nation coping with crisis. The remedy for bearing bad news or for exhaustion after long hours of work was 'a nice cuppa tea'. In the First World War rationing of

food did not begin until January 1918, when the tea ration was two ounces (56 grams) a week; coffee and other drinks were unrationed. But during the Second World War plans for food control had been made well in advance, and rationing of some items began within two months of the start of the war. Soon the tea ration was down to two ounces again.

Shortly after the First World War, the consumption of tea had reached over 8½ lbs (3.8 kilograms) per person per year while the figure for coffee was less than ¾ lb (340 grams). Probably the main reason for this difference was that tea was easy to brew, since it just required boiling water to be poured onto tea-leaves, while coffee had to be roasted, ground and brewed, which was quite a lengthy process for the ordinary housewife. If the British public were to be persuaded to drink coffee a simpler method of brewing would have to be found. In America in the 1890s a soluble dried coffee extract was developed, but the flavour was not satisfactory. A Japenese chemist also produced soluble tea and coffee, and several firms were supplying soluble coffee to the American forces in Europe during the First World War. A liquid sweetened coffee essence (Camp Coffee) was produced in Scotland and became quite popular. In 1938 Nestle's first introduced Nescafe, a spray-dried coffee, on the Continent, and a year later into Britain. The war delayed matters, but its story is one of the biggest post-war marketing successes.

Milk

Although milk had been recognized during the nineteenth century as a valuable source of nutrition, especially for children, the quality of milk had been so bad that until pasteurization was widely adopted it carried with it the serious risk of infection. However, the early years of the twentieth century saw increased concern about the high infant mortality rate, and the conviction that malnutrition was a major contributor to this problem. A number of 'milk depots' were therefore opened by local authorities and voluntary societies, where sterilized milk was supplied and advice given on the health of babies. During the First World War and between the wars, infant welfare centres grew unevenly through the country. However, the prevalence of bad teeth and rickets — both conditions due to inadequate calcium in the diet which could have been remedied by milk — pointed to the need for a more comprehensive child nutrition policy. By 1938 there were over 3,500 welfare centres in England and Wales where dried milk and other products were supplied at reduced prices, or free in cases of need.

In 1920 a National Milk Publicity Council was set up to run a campaign 'to make known in the interests of the nation the value of pure milk'. 'Milk Weeks' and lectures were organized, posters designed and displayed, and money spent on advertising in the press. However, the Council worked on a very modest budget. Some local authorities ran 'school milk clubs' and a number of

53 Farmers paste up some early milk publicity posters (1934).

54 The Minister of Agriculture photographed among enthusiastic supporters for the Milk in Schools Scheme.

nutrition experts published evidence about the value of milk for children's health. The Council linked milk publicity with success in sport and feats of endurance — boxers like Jack Dempsey, athletes like Johnnie Weismuller, and the aviator Colonel Lindbergh all testified to the benefits of milk. In 1928 Cambridge trained on milk and won the Boat Race!

Another successful idea was the Milk Bar. The first one, the Black and White Milk Bar, opened in Fleet Street, London, in 1935; it served between 150 and 200 different milk drinks. Soon there were a number of milk bars throughout the country, especially at holiday resorts. The Milk Council found that in 1920 the average amount of milk consumed per person in Britain was about two pints (1.1 litres) a week; by 1939 the figure had reached three pints (1.7) litres a week.

A happy accident contributed to the improved nutrition of schoolchildren. In the 1930s national over-production of milk created a problem which the government solved in 1934 by introducing the Milk in Schools Scheme. Children in state schools received one-third of a pint of milk a day at school at the subsidized price of ½d, or free in the case of hardship. The scheme was a great success, and by 1939 more than half of the nation's school-children were drinking the cheap milk. However, the scheme was of no benefit to most of the under-fives who did not go to school, so the government urged local authorities to buy milk at special cheap rates from the Milk Marketing Board and supply it cheaply or free to mothers and young children of families with low incomes. Not many authorities, however, took this advice. But in June 1940, five days after the evacuation from Dunkirk, the War Cabinet approved the National Milk Scheme which would cost the taxpayer £7½ million a year.

The National Milk Scheme entitled all children under five years of age and all expectant and nursing mothers to one pint of milk a day for 2d (the current price was 4½d) or free in case of need. The scheme was run through local offices of the Ministry of Food and the government footed the bill. There was no taint of charity about these arrangements which applied to all, and gave clear recognition of the need to give priority to mothers and babies in time of distress and difficulty. The scheme was an immediate success. By September 1940, 70 per cent of the 3½ million mothers and children eligible for the subsidized milk were receiving it, and 30 per cent of these were getting it free. There was also the alternative of 'national dried milk' for babies. By 1945 nearly four million mothers and young children were obtaining liquid or dried milk under the National Milk Scheme, but now only three per cent needed to get it free. The Milk in Schools Scheme was extended during the war to all school-children, and a Milk Cocoa Drink Scheme was introduced for adolescents at work. It was a remarkable achievement of the farmers of Britain that they were able to increase total milk production to provide for these schemes at a time when imports of animal feeding stuffs were greatly reduced.

10. Since 1945

Tea, Coffee Bars and Instant Coffee

Post-war Britain has been described as 'morally great but economically bankrupt', meaning that we had won the war, had high ideals for a better world in peacetime, but were hampered by lack of money and resources. When victory came, some people thought that all the wartime shortages would disappear overnight. In fact, however, far from being able to abolish food rationing, for instance, the government was forced to introduce bread rationing which had never been needed during the war. Milk rationing, which had begun in 1941, remained in operation until 1950; in 1948 the basic allowance was 2 pints (1.1 litres) a week per person, although there were still special amounts for mothers and children under the National Milk and the Milk in Schools Schemes.

Tea rationing ended in 1952 — it was not until seven years after the end of the war that we could drink as many cups of tea as we wanted! And by this time those interested in selling tea had become aware that coffee, which had never been rationed, was gaining in popularity, especially among young people. The publicity of the Milk Marketing Board led to competition from milk, and the increasing popularity of soft drinks made further inroads into the consumption of our national beverage. Nevertheless we were consuming nearly 9 lbs (4 kilograms) of tea per person each year. One post-war development was the use of tea bags, which have recently amounted to more than 10 per cent of the retail market and are gaining in popularity all the time. Purists claim that they do not make such a good cup of tea, but they have advantages for the busy housewife. Instant tea was another post-war idea but it has never been a success in this country, except for its limited use in vending machines.

While the post-war years saw some falling off in the demand for tea, there were at the same time great changes in the coffee trade. Foreign travel and foreign visitors led to a demand for a higher standard of coffee (which previously had often been lamentable) in cafés and restaurants, and as a result better methods of storing and brewing coffee began to be adopted. Coffee-drinking in fact was becoming fashionable again. There followed a boom in coffee bars, and then a huge growth in the sales of instant coffee. In 1970 consumption of coffee reached the figure of 3½ lbs (1.5 kilograms) per head (as compared with 0.88 lbs in 1939), while tea fell to just over 8 lbs (3.6 kilograms). Four-fifths of this coffee was processed into instant coffee, and a large proportion of the remaining fifth went to hotels and restaurants; only a small amount of ground coffee was used in the home.

55 (*Left*) Coffee bars were popular with young people as places where they could meet their friends.

56 (*Right*) Children help themselves to hot drinks from this vending machine installed in their school.

The vogue for coffee bars began in 1952. The first one opened in Soho, London, and then they sprang up throughout London and the provinces; by 1960 there were over 2,000 of them, 500 in the Greater London area alone. Coffee was mostly made in imported Italian espresso machines, big chromium-plated pieces of equipment that efficiently produced fresh cups of coffee for each customer by steam pressure. The Italian names of the coffee made in the new machines quickly slipped into the language — black coffee was called espresso and white coffee, in which the milk was heated and frothed up by hot steam, was called cappuccino, because it was the same colour as the habits of Capuchin friars. Most of the coffee bars had attractive contemporary decoration and a friendly, informal atmosphere. Just as the coffee reflected the standards of Italy or France so the food served in the coffee bars had a continental flavour, with open sandwiches, pizzas and French and Danish pastries. The coffee bars were especially popular among young people for whom they provided much-needed meeting places, and many of them had juke boxes. They were equally attractive to office workers at lunchtime, shoppers, students, tourists or businessmen who wanted a quick snack. Just as the coffee houses of the early eighteenth century had filled a social need for middle-class men about town, so the coffee bars over two hundred years later met the needs of a wide range of people who could now get attractively-presented light refreshments and a non-alcoholic drink at reasonable prices and in relaxed surroundings. Twenty years after the first coffee bars opened the novelty has worn off, and often the standard of the coffee has declined. The fault lies not in the coffee machines, but in the quality and the quantity of the ground coffee used. Nevertheless, the boom in coffee bars introduced many of the British public to coffee, and made them interested enough to make it for themselves at home.

As was mentioned earlier, the introduction of instant coffee into Britain was delayed because of the outbreak of the Second World War. The first sort of instant coffee was spray-dried coffee, which is made in giant percolators, three storeys high; they produce liquid coffee under pressure which is then turned into powder in stainless steel dryers. The two big rivals at first were Nescafe and Maxwell House. Then, in the 1960s, accelerated freeze-dried instant coffee was developed, which produced coffee in larger granules than the spray-dried coffee, and which smelled and tasted more like 'real' coffee. Unfortunately, however, the new method is an expensive process, so that the granular coffee is dearer than the powdered sort.

Drink-Vending Machines

Coin-operated machines date back to very early times. In 215 BC Hero, a mathematician who lived in Alexandria, described a machine for dispensing sacrificial water in Egyptian temples. One of the first machines to supply hot drinks was patented in London in 1895 by a man called Robinson. It made use of waste heat from the street gas lamps to heat water for drinks. An elaborate lamp was put up at the corner of Leicester Square in 1898 which dispensed cocoa, coffee and beef tea. It was so popular that crowds caused serious obstruction and the owners of the machine were asked to remove it.

The invention of the paper cup early in the twentieth century opened the way for further developments in drink-vending machines. In the 1930s Coca-Cola and other soft-drink firms were selling bottled drinks from refrigerated machines. During the war, progress in the machines was held up in Britain until it was discovered that they were a useful device for helping war workers to keep going for long hours. Soon machines had been installed in some factories. The boom in drink-vending machines, however, did not begin until the 1950s. The Milk Marketing Board gave its blessing to an experimental machine at Paddington Station which sold 1,754 half-pint cartons of chilled milk in one week. Machines that would produce acceptable hot tea and coffee were the next problem, and various methods of using leaf tea and ground coffee, liquid concentrates and powdered instant tea and coffee were tried out. By the 1960s the machines were widely used in industry and offices, though where the workers were given any choice they definitely still preferred a tea-lady with a trolley of drinks. Tea-ladies' drinks, however, are infinitely more expensive for the employers to provide so there has been a steady move towards machines. The machines are now so much accepted by the general public that we might wonder how we ever did without them.

57 (*Left*) Publicity about milk tailored to fit in with the campaign against drinking and driving.

58 (*Right*) Dead fish killed by toxic waste float in the River Seine in France. Pollution of rivers and water supplies has become a cause of great public concern.

Milk

By 1953 the average weekly consumption of milk had reached 5 pints (2.8 litres) per head per week (from 2 pints in 1920 and 3 pints in 1939) without any special publicity efforts. The reason for this was that there was little unemployment and poverty, and housewives who were aware of the value of milk for their families were able to pay for it. Mothers had probably themselves benefited from the pre-war milk in schools and had acquired a taste for milk. However, the National Milk Publicity Council believed that they could greatly increase milk consumption if they embarked on a modern, enterprising selling campaign. The old slogan 'Drink More Milk' had little bite but in 1954 they discovered a personality, Zoë Newton, to typify the health and vitality that drinking milk would bring. Soon posters of this vivacious, attractive girl created a national personality, and a campaign of films, recipes, diets, cookery demonstrations, posters, information for schools, and other publicity was under way. In spite of the government's reduced subsidy on milk which caused the retail price to go up by 14 per cent in only six months, milk sales recovered from the initial blow and began to rise again. In 1954 consumption of milk was 53 per cent above that of pre-war days and was rising steadily. Between 1954 and 1957 milk drinking by adults increased by about 25 per cent while young adults (16–30) were drinking twice as much as they had been three years before.

Then in 1958 came the birth of one of the most effective slogans of all time — 'Drinka Pinta Milka Day'. The catchy advice appeared on hoardings all over

87

the country and was followed by a varied publicity campaign. Liquid milk sales increased but not as quickly as had been hoped because again there was a rise in price. Milk was still, however, a 'good buy' — it took the average working man nearly twelve minutes to earn the price of a pint of milk in 1938, but in 1964 in took him only six minutes. In 1967 annual sales of milk were 140 million gallons higher than in 1957. However, in 1968 the government decided that the Milk in Schools Scheme was unnecessary for secondary school children at this time of general prosperity and that they could save £4 million a year by not paying for the 15 million gallons involved. Milk was, however, still to be supplied to younger children at school, and be available cheaply for babies and expectant and nursing mothers.

Water

With our rainy climate it seems absurd that Britain could suffer from a shortage of water, but it is a fact that we are facing a water crisis. Our consumption of water has doubled over the last 50 years, and during the next 25 years our needs are likely to double again. Clearly, we will have to become much more water-conscious and to think of ways of cutting down consumption. There has even been recent discussion in Parliament about fitting meters and charging domestic and industrial users according to the amount of water they use. Another serious problem is that of pollution of surface and underground water from waste from factories and houses. For instance the widespread use of detergents has caused masses of froth in rivers and the large-scale destruction of fish and other natural life. Protection of the environment is a popular cause of public concern, and conservation of water and prevention of its pollution are an important part of this campaign. In the past water supplies were organized by a hotch-potch of different local authorities, but now there are large Regional Boards who will be able to plan more efficiently, while the Department of the Environment is responsible centrally for maintaining a pure and plentiful water supply.

Recent Changes in Drinking Habits

The present century has seen continuous change in drinking habits. The very heavy beer-drinking contrasted with extreme temperance of the pre-First World War years has largely disappeared. The dreary beer-swilling public houses with spitoons and sawdust on the floor, into which no lady would enter, have gone, and have been replaced by socially acceptable centres for food, drink and entertainment. Although it is illegal to serve children with alcoholic drinks, or for them to enter premises serving such drinks, many public houses now have gardens or playrooms for children. There is pressure in some quarters to change the law so that families can drink alcoholic and soft drinks together in the manner of the Continental café. Some public houses in turn are offering their customers coffee as an alternative beverage.

There has been a great increase in the sales of soft drinks in recent years, partly because people are more prosperous and can afford such inessential items, and partly because this prosperity means that more people have refrigerators which make fruit squashes and fizzy drinks more attractive. Fizzy drinks are made by pumping carbon dioxide into the drink which is usually given a fruit or other flavour such as lemonade, coca cola, ginger beer, tonic water, etc. All fizzy drinks have to be kept in sealed bottles or cans as they become flat if the gas escapes. Soft drinks have a large amount of sugar in them, and it has been a cause of concern that children drink so many of them which has a bad effect on their teeth. Alternative sweeteners such as cyclamates and saccharine have also been used, but these too are believed to present certain health risks.

Sales of bottled and canned beer have greatly increased, since many people now prefer to drink in their own homes — again refrigeration helps — perhaps watching television programmes rather than going out to the 'pub'. There are complaints from beer-drinkers that draught beer is not what it used to be. Now, instead of fermenting for a length of time in the wood, the process is speeded up and the beer is then sterilized so that the fermenting agents are killed. Chemicals are added to improve the taste, but those who knew the beers of the past are often dissatisfied with the new brewing standards. In response to this, pressure groups such as the 'Preservation of Beer from the Wood Society' have grown up, campaigning against the use of the oxygen-pump in serving beer, and for a return to the non-pressurized natural beers from wooden tuns. In 1963

59 (*Left*) A volunteer taking the breath test is watched by a member of the Road Research Laboratory.

60 (*Right*) Two victims of the disease of alcoholism.

Excise restrictions on brewing beer at home were abolished in Britain. Since beers and stouts can now be brewed very cheaply at home, there has been a great vogue for home-brewing. Complete home-brewing kits can be bought at many shops, and as a result bathrooms and spare rooms all over the country have been seething with home-brews maturing, as was the custom in the Middle Ages. Home-made wine is also popular.

Another great change in British drinking habits is the taste for wine that has grown up, probably as a result of the increase in holidays abroad. Wine importing and sale used to be a very specialized affair, with carefully-selected 'Château bottled' wines, and much expertise about vintages and the like. Now wine-drinking is not just for the wealthy and knowledgeable but also for ordinary people who want wines for everyday drinking (French *vins ordinaires*). No doubt Britain's entry into the Common Market will increase further the booming trade in wine. We can now buy our wines in big wine chain-stores, grocers and supermarkets, and there is keen price-cutting competition in this rapidly expanding trade. 'Beaujolais' and 'Burgundy' are now more familiar labels in the supermarket than such English drinks of bygone times as ginger beer, perry or mead.

The Dangers of Alcohol

Although the heavy working-class beer-drinking of the early twentieth century has declined, there are still serious problems arising from over-indulgence in alcoholic drink. One hazard, as the ownership of cars has multiplied, has been drunken driving. In 1967, Mrs Barbara Castle, who was then Minister of Transport, introduced legislation to protect the public against this danger. Police were allowed to 'breathalyze' any driver whose control of his car made them suspect that he had had too much to drink. The breathalyzer is a simple device into which a driver is asked to blow; if the chemical in the device turns green it indicates that alcohol over the legal maximum has probably been taken. A more exact test can be made at the police station with blood or urine samples. After this new measure was introduced, there was a marked reduction in the number of accidents.

Another serious problem is that of alcoholism, a chronic disease in which the sufferer has an uncontrollable desire for alcohol. Once the craving for alcohol has been triggered off, the subject is addicted and cannot stop drinking. Not all heavy drinkers are alcoholics. Some who drink a great deal can nevertheless stop at will, whereas the alcoholic is 'hooked' and dependent on alcohol. There are probably between 300,000 and 500,000 alcoholics in Great Britain, and this is a relatively low proportion of the population as compared with countries such as the USA or France.

One way in which society can try to control excessive drinking is by regulating the price of drink, and by imposing strict licensing laws. A survey in

Canada has shown that the incidence of cirrhosis of the liver (a disease which is caused by excessive drinking of alcohol) is directly related to the price of alcohol and the level of wages. In the eighteenth century the government had to step in with measures of this kind to control the epidemic of gin-drinking. Now there are heavy taxes on all alcoholic drink, and its sale is restricted to licensed premises with limited hours of opening.

A voluntary society called Alcoholics Anonymous has helped thousands of once-addicted people to learn to live without alcohol. This is done by sympathy, and advice from people who themselves have been alcoholics. There are also hospitals and clinics which work like Alcoholics Anonymous, and provide group therapy, and also psychotherapy and drug treatment. One of the saddest groups in modern society are the down-and-out alcoholics, who are addicted to alcohol but cannot afford ordinary drink and so drink methyl-alcohol, which is present in methylated and surgical spirit, a very poisonous substance which can cause blindness and even death.

Alcohol then is something of a mixed blessing. To the wine connoisseur it is 'life-enhancing'; combined with good food and good company, it can contribute relaxation and contentment to social relationships. Alcohol is, however, fairly high in calories so those who have weight problems need to watch what they drink as well as what they eat. Alcohol is usually believed to be a stimulant and make people who drink it more lively, but in fact it actually depresses the nerve centres of the brain, and impairs the powers of concentration, judgement and control. Drink tends to make us relax our inhibitions, and so gives the impression of being a stimulant; but soon it makes us sleepy. Alcohol taken in moderate quantities is a pleasant additive to life; taken in excess it is a killer on the roads, and produces that pathetic social casualty, the alcoholic.

List of Drinks

ALE   Made from malt, yeast and water. There are three main processes — (1) Malting. The barley is treated so that the starch changes into sugar. (2) Extracting. Once the starch has become sugar, the goodness is taken out in liquid form. (3) Fermenting. Yeast is added to the liquid and converts the sugar partly into alcohol and partly into carbon dioxide.

ANJOU   White and red table wines from the Anjou district of France.

APERITIF An appetiser, or drink which is supposed to stimulate the appetite.

AQUAVITAE A distilled spirit similar to crude gin.

BEAUJOLAIS A light fruity French red wine, usually drunk fairly 'young'.

BEER Made from malt, yeast, water and hops. The process is similar to making ale, but the hops make the drink more bitter.

BITTER A dry draught beer well-flavoured with hops.

BORDEAUX Red and white table wines from south-west France. Also known as Gascon wine.

BRANDY A spirit distilled from grape-wine. The word first used in the seventeenth century was originally 'brandwine' or 'brandewine' from the Dutch *brandewijn* meaning burned (or distilled) wine. Cognac is a famous French brandy.

BURGUNDY Rich red and white table wines from central France.

BUTTERMILK The liquid left after churning butter.

CHABLIS A dry white wine from the Burgundy area of France.

CHAMPAGNE Perhaps the greatest and certainly the best-known of the French sparkling white wines.

CHOCOLATE A hot drink made with water or milk and ground cacao seeds.

CIDER A drink made from fermented apple juice.

CLARET (from the French *clairet*) A clear red wine from the Bordeaux district of France.

CLARRY A sweet wine mixed with honey and spices, drunk in the Middle Ages.

COCA COLA A fizzy soft drink flavoured with nuts from the African cola tree.

COCKTAILS A mixture of spirits and other liquids (wines, liqueurs, fruit juice, etc) shaken with ice.

COCOA A hot drink made from ground cacao seeds and milk and/or water.

COFFEE A hot drink made from boiling water and the seeds (beans) of a shrub which have been roasted and ground. *Espresso coffee* – black coffee. *Cappuccino coffee* – coffee with frothed milk.

COGNAC see Brandy.

CORDIAL Aromatic or fruit-flavoured concentrated drink. Usually non-alcoholic. Added to water or to spirits.

FRUIT SQUASH Concentrated cordial or fruit-flavoured syrup to add to water or spirits.

GASCON see Bordeaux.

GIN A spirit distilled from corn and flavoured with juniper berries. Name derived from 'Geneva', from the Dutch or French name for juniper berries. Also known as 'Hollands',

GINGER BEER A fizzy 'soft' drink flavoured with ginger.

GROG A mixture of spirits (especially rum) and water.

HIPPOCRAS Made from red and white wine, herbs and spices, and strained through a 'Hippocrates sleeve', so called because it looked like the sleeve of an apothecary's gown.

HOCK   A fruity white wine from Germany.

LEMONADE   A 'soft' drink, either made with lemons, sugar and water, or a fizzy lemon-flavoured drink.

LIQUEUR   Distilled spirit mixed with honey or sugar, and herbs or fruit flavourings — eg Benedictine, Cherry Brandy, Chartreuse.

MADEIRA   A dessert wine fortified with brandy, from the Portuguese island of Madeira.

MEAD   An alcoholic drink made from fermented honey mixed with water and herbs. Also called hydromel (by Greeks and Romans) and metheglin (in Wales).

METHEGLIN   A Welsh form of mead, flavoured with herbs and spices.

MILD   A brown beer not strongly flavoured with hops.

NEGUS   Mulled wine or port, a mixture of wine, sugar and hot water.

NETTLE BEER   A fizzy 'soft' drink flavoured with nettles.

PERRY   A fermented drink made from the juice of pears.

POITOU   Table wines from western France.

PORT   A sweet dark red (occasionally white) fortified wine, shipped from the town of Oporto in Portugal, whence it gets its name.

PORTER   A dark-brown bitter beer brewed from browned malt, and especially popular in earlier times with market porters.

RUM   (originally called tafia) A distilled spirit from cane sugar or its products.

SCHNAPPS   A distilled spirit similar to a crude gin.

SELTZER   An aerated or fizzy mineral water from Germany.

SODA WATER   An effervescent water made by adding carbonic acid under pressure.

STOUT   A strong dark-brown beer brewed (especially in Dublin) with roasted malt.

TEA   A hot drink made from the infusion in boiling water of the leaves of a shrub of the camellia family. There are two main varieties — green and black tea.

TONIC WATER   A fizzy 'soft' drink flavoured with quinine.

VIN CUIT   Concentrated wine which was boiled down to about one-third of its original volume and flavoured with herbs and spices.

WHEY   The watery part of milk that has been separated from the curd.

WHISKY   A distilled spirit made from starch. The word is derived from the Gaelic phrase *uisge-beatha*, water of life. Scotch whisky is made from malted barley, some other whiskies are made from rye.

WINE   Made by the fermentation of grape-juice (or other fruits and even vegetables) during which sugar is transformed into alcohol. The process occurs naturally since yeast cells appear on the skin of the grape as it ripens.

Further Reading

As in the companion volume in this series on *Food* there are three basic source books that will be found most useful. They are: *The Englishman's Food* by J C Drummond and Anne Wilbraham (Cape, 1958), *Plenty and Want* by John Burnett (Penguin, 1968) and *A History of the Cost of Living* also by John Burnett (Penguin, 1969). There are also a number of helpful books on particular topics.

On beer, wines and spirits:
D & P Brothwell, *Food in Antiquity* (Thames and Hudson, 1969)
Andrew Campbell, *The Book of Beer* (Dennis Dobson).
Hugh Johnson, *Wine* (Sphere Books).
Charles Seltmann, *Wine in the Ancient World* (Methuen).
D Sutherland, *Raise Your Glasses* (Macdonald).
B C A Turner & C J J Berry, *The Winemakers Companion* (Mills & Boon).

On tea, coffee and chocolate:
Edward Bramah, *Tea and Coffee* (Hutchinson, 1972).
Denys Forrest, *Tea for the British* (Chatto & Windus, 1973).
H E Jacob, *The Saga of Coffee* (Allen & Unwin, 1935).

On water supplies:
D Davies, *Fresh Water* (Aldus, 1968).
Dorothy Hartley, *Water in England* (Macdonald, 1964).
J P M Pannell, *An Illustrated History of Civil Engineering* (Thames and Hudson, 1964).

On milk:
A Jenkins, *Drinka Pinta* (Heinemann, 1970).

On the Temperance Movement:
J C Furnas, *The Life and Times of the Late Demon Rum* (W H Allen, 1965).
B Harrison, *Drink and the Victorians* (Faber, 1971).
N Longmate, *The Water Drinkers* (Hamish Hamilton, 1968).

Index

The numbers in **bold** refer to the figure numbers of illustrations.

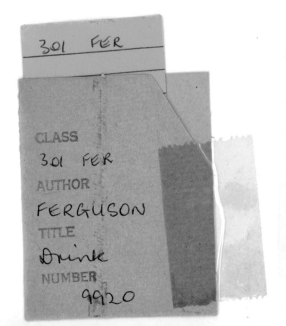